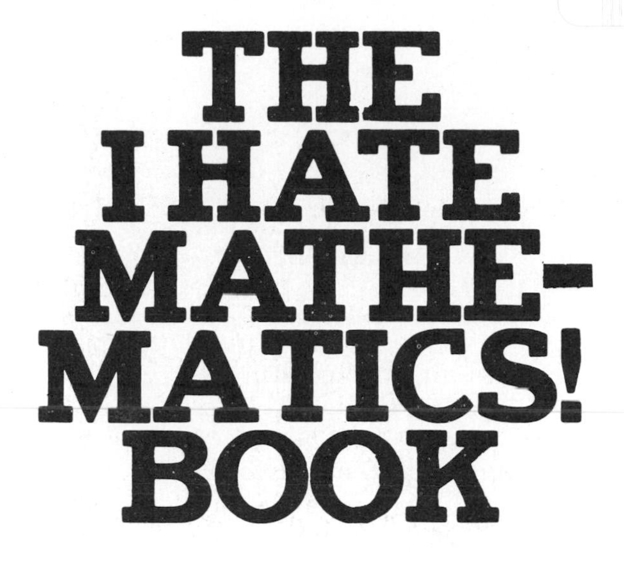

THE I HATE MATHEMATICS! BOOK

by

Marilyn Burns

illustrated by

Martha Hairston

CAMBRIDGE UNIVERSITY PRESS
Cambridge
New York Port Chester
Melbourne Sydney

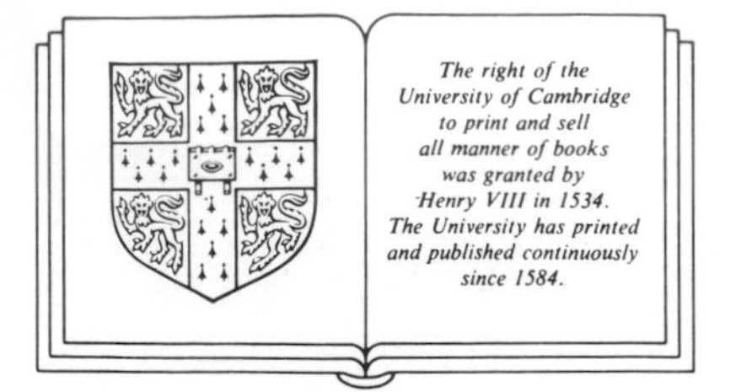

Published by the Press Syndicate of the University of Cambridge
The Pitt Building, Trumpington Street, Cambridge CB2 1RP
40 West 20th Street, New York, NY 10011, USA
10 Stamford Road, Oakleigh, Melbourne 3166, Australia

This version first published by Cambridge University Press 1987
Fourth printing 1990

Adaptation by Sue Glover

Printed in Great Britain by Scotprint Ltd, Musselburgh, Scotland

British Library cataloguing in publication data

Burns, Marilyn
The I hate mathematics! book.

1. Mathematics—Juvenile literature
I. Title II. Hairston, Martha
510 QA40.5

ISBN 0 521 33414 4 hard covers
ISBN 0 521 33659 7 paperback

What's in This Book

Starting Out Right

Some of the nicest people hate mathematics.
Especially kids who think mathematics = arithmetic.
Here are some of the things they say:

"I hate mathematics so much it makes me sick!"
"Mathematics is for sissies."
"Mathematics is impossible!"
"People who like mathematics are really gross."
"Mathematicians have little pig eyes."
"What good is it anyway?"

Now go and write down your own favourite anti-mathematics slogan.
Make it good!

This book is about how to change from a mathematical weakling into a mathematical heavyweight.

You can impress your teachers
reassure your family
earn new respect from your friends
dazzle yourself.

Because nobody *likes* to hate mathematics.

How will this miracle be accomplished, you ask?

Will we use tricks? Or fancy talk?
Or threats? Or fun and games?

YES!

(but there is a secret to it) and here it is:

It's not hard and it isn't boring.
It just takes a bit of reorganization of what is already in your head
(you don't even always need a pencil).

YOU ARE A MATHEMATICAL GENIUS IN DISGUISE!

Here is how to prove it in 1 easy step:
read the rest of this book.

P.S. The password of mathematics is *pattern*.

Street Maths

What to do when:

There's no school,
your mother made you go
out of the house for the day because she wanted to clean,
and even gave you a sandwich for lunch,
your friend has gone away for the weekend,
your best ball has just exploded,
it's too hot to run around,
you already ate the sandwich and it's only 10 o'clock,
you definitely feel ready to try something new.

Here are some ways to take a mathematical look
at your neighbourhood:
Experiments with whatever passes through.
Investigations of what's always been there.
Suggestions for mathematical conversations
with passers-by, wise guys and sceptics.

You might want to try some
even if your friend *doesn't* go away for the weekend.

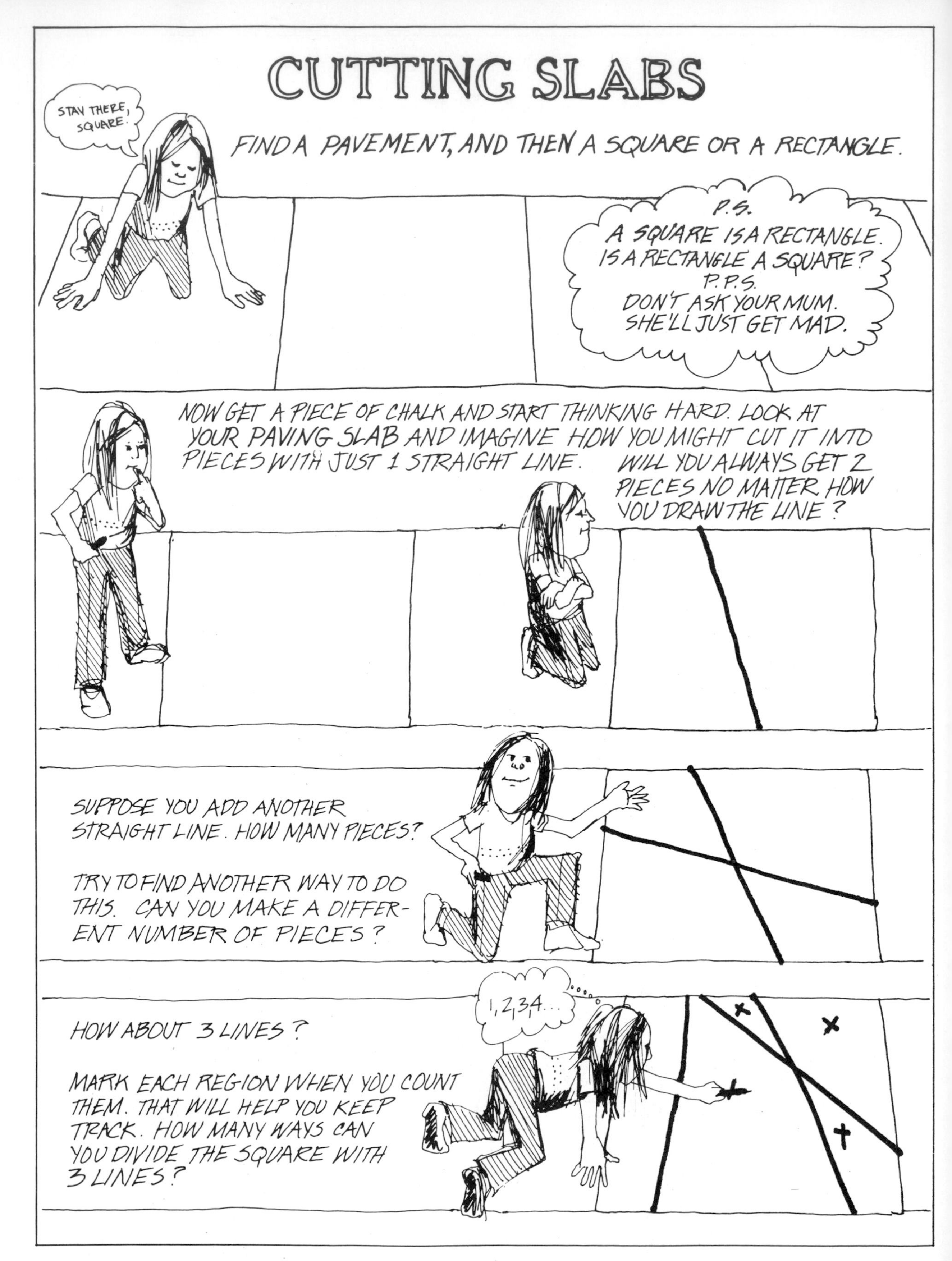
CUTTING SLABS
STAY THERE, SQUARE.
FIND A PAVEMENT, AND THEN A SQUARE OR A RECTANGLE.
P.S.
A SQUARE IS A RECTANGLE.
IS A RECTANGLE A SQUARE?
P.P.S.
DON'T ASK YOUR MUM.
SHE'LL JUST GET MAD.
NOW GET A PIECE OF CHALK AND START THINKING HARD. LOOK AT YOUR PAVING SLAB AND IMAGINE HOW YOU MIGHT CUT IT INTO PIECES WITH JUST 1 STRAIGHT LINE.
WILL YOU ALWAYS GET 2 PIECES NO MATTER HOW YOU DRAW THE LINE?
SUPPOSE YOU ADD ANOTHER STRAIGHT LINE. HOW MANY PIECES?
TRY TO FIND ANOTHER WAY TO DO THIS. CAN YOU MAKE A DIFFERENT NUMBER OF PIECES?
1,2,3,4...
HOW ABOUT 3 LINES?
MARK EACH REGION WHEN YOU COUNT THEM. THAT WILL HELP YOU KEEP TRACK. HOW MANY WAYS CAN YOU DIVIDE THE SQUARE WITH 3 LINES?

NOW YOU'RE READY FOR THE BIG TIME.
FOUR LINES! (GOT YOUR CHALK?)
SEVEN!
SEVEN WHAT?
Hup! two! three! four!
step on a crack, break yer mother's back.
FIVE!
EIGHT!

WHAT IS THE SMALLEST NUMBER OF REGIONS YOU CAN MAKE?

WHAT IS THE LARGEST NUMBER?

CAN YOU DO ALL THE ONES IN BETWEEN?

HOW MANY WAYS CAN YOU FIND TO MAKE 5 REGIONS?
Remember, no lines like this→

HOW ABOUT TRYING TO CUT A PAVING SLAB WITH 5 LINES? 6 LINES?

HOW ABOUT A HOLDING A CONTEST TO FIND THE MOST REGIONS FOR 10 LINES?

WHAT WOULD HAPPEN IF YOU COULD CURVE THE LINES?

A LINE IS FOREVER

To a mathematician, a line has no beginning and no end. It goes on forever.

What we draw are *line segments*. They start somewhere and end somewhere. Even mathematicians can only draw line segments. What about road markings? Are they lines or line segments?

CUTTING YOUR CAKE
(AND EATING YOUR BROTHER'S PIECE TOO)

Partitioning (cutting up things with line segments) has interested lots of mathematicians. Maybe it will interest your brother too. Next time your mother makes a kind of cake you like a lot, bet your brother his piece that you can get 11 pieces from only 4 straight cuts across the cake. Then eat and run!

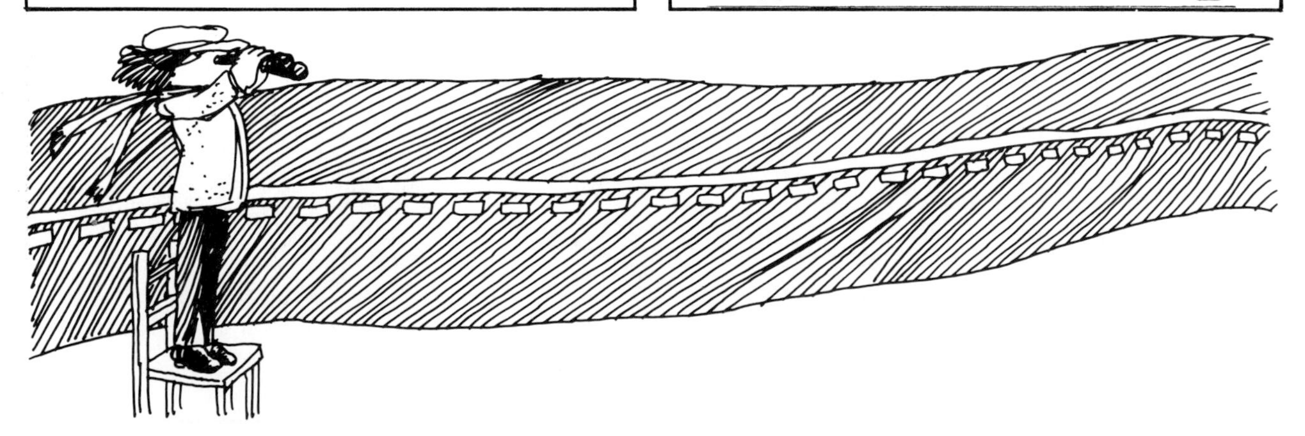

THINGS TO DO IN A PHONE BOX

(while you're waiting for a bus and it's raining)

Back in the olden days, people used to think it was fun to squash a whole lot of folks into a phone box and have their pictures taken. (In the olden days people had weird ideas.) How many kids your size would fit into a phone box?

If you think that might cause trouble, try this variation. Some evening when you have fruit salad for dinner, see how many grapes you can fit into your mouth at once.

Or, how many circus clowns can fit into a taxi if they are late and in a big hurry?

What is the smallest size cube you could squeeze yourself into? One with sides of 50 cm? 75 cm? 100 cm?
(What's another name for the last cube?)

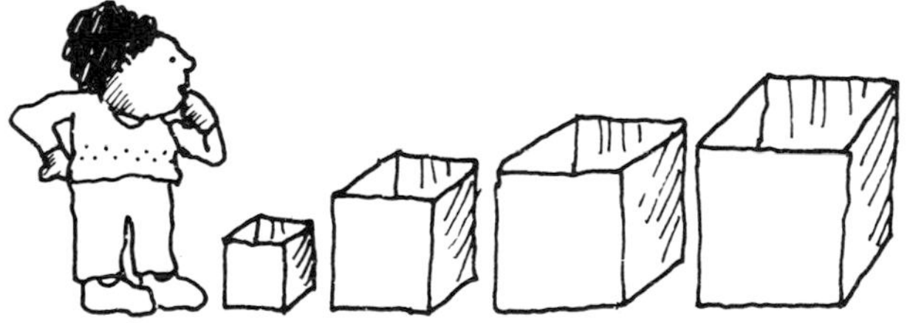

ALL THESE QUESTIONS ARE ABOUT **VOLUME**. THAT'S MATHEMATICS FOR HOW MUCH SPACE SOMETHING TAKES UP.

Meanwhile, back in the phone box . . .

How many names are in the phone book? A thousand? A million? Make a guess. Then check to see. Do you have to count every one?

How many telephone numbers can there be that start with the same first 3 numbers as yours? Is this one of those trick questions?

GETTING CLOSE TO PIGEONS

HOW CLOSE WILL PIGEONS LET YOU GET? ARE SOME PIGEONS SHYER THAN OTHERS? CAN YOU MAKE A PREDICTION ABOUT HOW CLOSE PIGEONS WILL USUALLY LET YOU GET BEFORE THEY FLY AWAY OR MOVE? TRY THIS EXPERIMENT:

1. Pick a pigeon.

2. Walk slowly towards it. Try not to make any sudden movements or loud noises. Try to look inconspicuous.

3. When it flies away or moves, drop a key ring.*

4. Keep your eye on the spot where the pigeon was. Measure the distance from there to the key ring.

*KEY RINGS MAKE GOOD MARKERS BECAUSE THEY DON'T BOUNCE OR ROLL AWAY WHEN YOU DROP THEM. BUT YOU CAN USE ANYTHING THAT WORKS THE SAME WAY.

5. Do this at least 10 times.

6. Is there a pattern? What is the average fright distance of pigeons in your neighbourhood?

If you don't know any pigeons personally, try seagulls. Or robins.
If you don't know any birds personally, try people. See the next page.
Do bread crumbs or sunflower seeds change the results you get (with birds)?

What does all this have to do with mathematics?

GETTING CLOSE TO PEOPLE

You'll probably find it's easier to get close to pigeons. But after you've had a little experience with birds (or if you can't find any birds), you might do the same experiment with people.

The trick is what to do while you're inching up on them. With birds you don't have to do anything but look nonchalant. That might not work with people. Here are 2 suggestions:

1.

Don't tell them what you're doing. Instead, start talking about something that will give you time to move very slowly toward them. Make it convincing. When your subject begins to look uncomfortable, or backs off, *then* tell them, and take a measurement.

2.

Or you could tell them what your experiment is first. And ask them to tell you when they begin to *feel* like you're too close. Then measure.

Are people shyer than birds?

Are men shyer than women?

Are grownups shyer than kids?

STREET CRACKERY

Do you ever walk down the street and try not to step on *any* cracks? Or try to step on *every* crack? Which takes more steps? What happens if you just walk normally? Make a prediction about what you think would happen. This is called a *hypothesis.*

Here's an experiment to do to test your prediction. You'll need enough spare time to walk up and down the street 4 times.

Pick a street with a fairly regular pavement pattern.

1

Walk along the street normally and count how many steps it takes. Write it down.

2

Now walk back normally again and count how many cracks you step on. Write this down.

3

Now walk back again, making sure to step on every crack. Count your steps and write the total down.

4

Once more now, walk, avoiding every crack. Walk as normally as possible. Change the length of your pace only to avoid cracks. Count your steps again and record.

What conclusion can you draw? If anyone looks at you funny or makes any kind of smart remark, like:

Just say:

Never miss a chance to mathematically dazzle wise guys.

WHY NOT SHOELACES?

Ever find yourself thinking about shoelaces? You might be minding your own business, doing nothing in particular, and all of a sudden you start thinking about shoelaces. Then you start *noticing* shoelaces. Strings tied to people's feet! And the longer you look, the funnier it seems.

That's when to do a shoelace survey. How many shoes have laces? Half? More than half? Less than half? First, make a prediction.

Then find a pencil and paper and a place to sit where you can concentrate on feet.

Make a chart that looks like this:

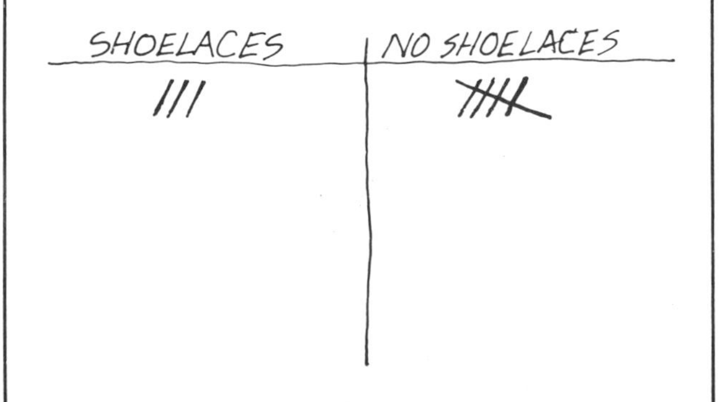

If you have picked a busy corner or you try this at rush hour at the subway exit, you may have to get a friend to help. (One looks, the other tallies.)

Stick with it. The bigger your sample, the more accurate your survey.

Do it until you think you have enough.

Or until it's too dark and you have to go home.

Or until you get so hungry you can't stand it another minute.

Was your prediction right?

Would it be the same if you only counted men's shoes? Or just women's? Would it be different at some other time of year? (Do wellingtons have laces?)

So you don't think shoelaces are so terrific? Try hats. Or neckties.

Make a guess: how many people will have to walk by until you see a woman pushing a pram and wearing a red sweater?

And if someone says:

"Hey, kid! What're you doing down there? Lose your money down the drain?"

Just say:

"I'm taking a mathematical shoelace sample. What percentage of shoes do *you* think have laces?"

If they don't answer, they probably wouldn't know a *statistic* if it walked up and said, "Hello!" A statistic is what you have when you say something like:

"Just 43 per cent of the people on High St. today were wearing shoes with laces."

Mathematicians eat ice cream just like everyone else. But sometimes they don't wait in line like everyone else. See the mathematician in this picture? She's the one holding up the line. That's because she is thinking. About ice cream. Actually, about double scoop ice cream cones. She's trying to figure out how many possible double scoop cones there are if there are 31 famous flavours to choose from.

Now that's a real problem!

It has to do with things called "permutations" and "combinations." If you think it doesn't matter which flavour is on top and which is on the bottom, then you're talking about *combinations.*

But if you think that a double scoop ice cream cone with jamoca almond fudge on top and strawberry on the bottom is *not* the same as strawberry on the top and jamoca almond fudge on the bottom, then you're talking about *permutations.*

There is a big difference.

It's easier to start with a smaller number. What are your 3 most favourite flavours? Pistachio, chocolate mint, and rum raisin? Okay. How many different combinations are there? How about permutations? Hint: until you've done this a little, it may help to draw a picture.

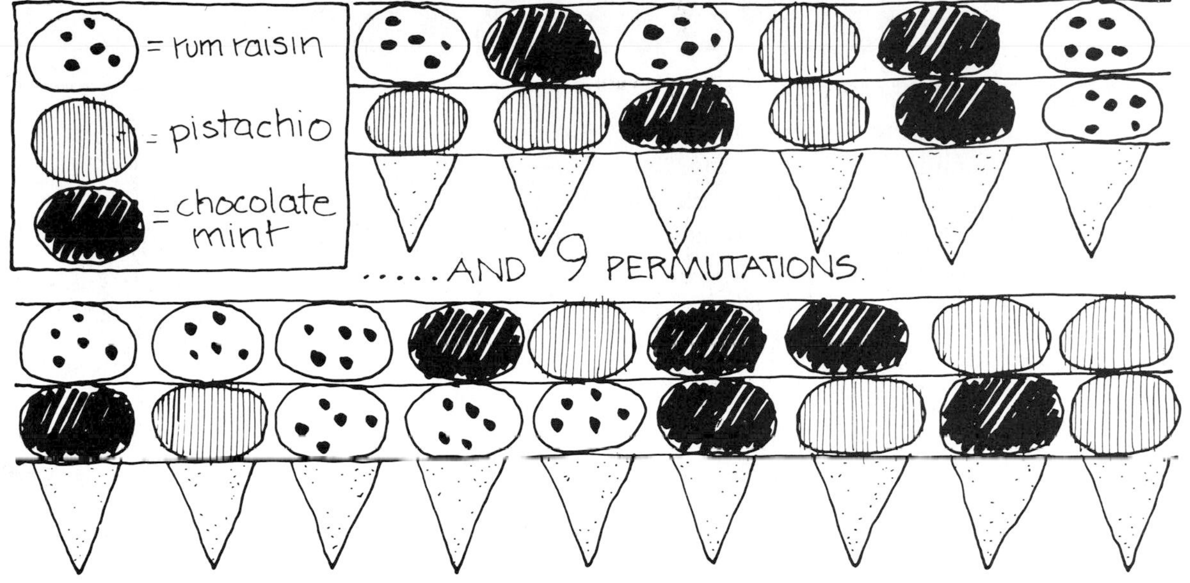

Now do a little research at the nearest ice cream shop. Figure out how many different possibilities there are for the flavours they sell. (Stick with combinations.) After you've figured it out, see if you can win yourself a free cone by betting the ice cream man he can't guess how many combinations there are. If he tells you to get lost, try it with one of your friends. Or your big brother.

WHAT KIND OF BORING PERSON GETS VANILLA DOUBLE DIPS?

ARE YOU A COMBINATION CONE-EATER OR A PERMUTATION CONE-EATER?

WHAT HAPPENS IF YOU HAVE TO CHOOSE BETWEEN A CONE AND A SUNDAE?

WITH A FLAKE? WITH SYRUP?

ARGHHH!

DO YOU MAKE THICK MILK SHAKES?

HOW MANY HANDSHAKES?

Suppose you walk down to the corner some afternoon and there are 6 of your friends standing around. How many handshakes would there be? Zero handshakes because normal kids don't shake hands? Okay, but just suppose you did. You each shake hands with everyone once. How many?

Try it. Do it sometime when you're at the corner anyway, waiting for the bus, and there isn't anything special to do and you want to take your mind off the fact that this morning your mum said she was cooking liver for dinner and don't be late. How many handshakes?

There is a mathematical pattern even in handshakes! And here is how a mathematician would look for it. He would say:

This mathematician's Hmmm-Aha! method could be written out in shorthand like this:

Hmmm. (People)	Aha! (Handshakes)
1	0
2	1
3	
4	
5	

Continue the pattern and see if it helps you to predict what would happen at the corner if there were 10 friends there.

MORE LOGICAL THINKING (or, there is egg on your face!)

HERE IS ANOTHER ONE OF THOSE QUESTIONS THAT SOUNDS LIKE A TRICK UNTIL YOU REALIZE IT'S REALLY PRACTICE IN STRAIGHT THINKING.

A TOPOLOGICAL GARDEN

A topological garden is *not* one of those places where they grow weird plants that have long names you can't pronounce. A topological garden can be any place at all, because *topology* is a part of mathematics. Topology is the study of surfaces.

If you can peel an orange and keep the skin in *1 piece* you have solved a topological problem.

CAN YOU DO IT?

Here is another one. This has to do with lines connecting points. Pick 1 place you walk to all the time. Like the playground. Or a friend's house. Chances are you go the same way each time, right? But here is what a topologist who is interested in lines connecting points might say:

NO MORE WALKING THE SAME OLD WAY FOR ME!

TOPOLOGIST INTERESTED IN LINES CONNECTING POINTS.

And here's what else such a mathematician might say:

Actually, there is no telling what else such a mathematician might say.

Try it yourself.

Choose a place to walk to.

Count how many streets you cross the way you usually go.

Can you get there by crossing fewer streets?

Try it crossing twice as many.

But don't cross any twice.

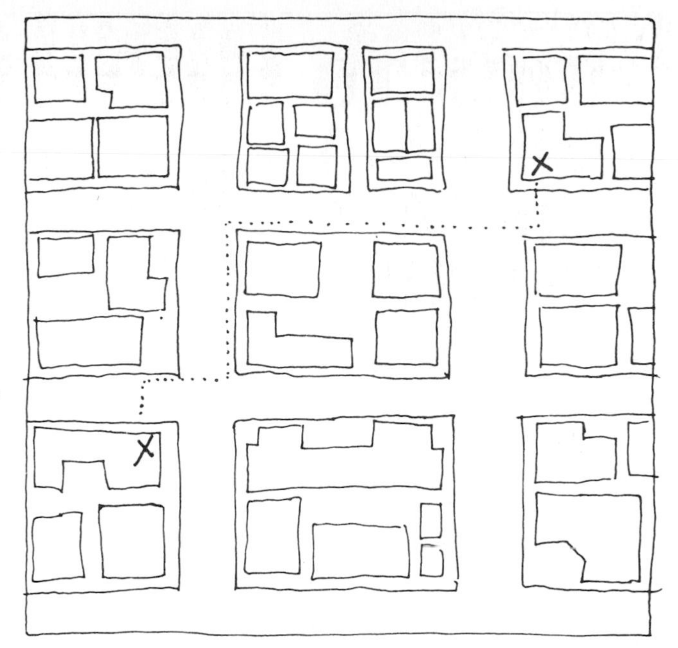

And when some big kid asks what you're doing in his neighbourhood, just tell him you're a topologist doing an investigation in *network theory*. Stand tall. And walk briskly.

Can you walk through all the doors in your house once before walking through any a second time? P.S. Can you do it *without* getting in trouble?

Put a point somewhere near the middle of this drawing. Is it on the inside or the outside? Topologists would find out by drawing a line from the point to the outside, and then counting the times the line crosses the drawing. If it crosses an odd number, the point is inside. Do you know why?

HOW TO DRAW A CROWD WITHOUT STARTING A FIGHT

(OR GETTING INTO TROUBLE OF ANY KIND)

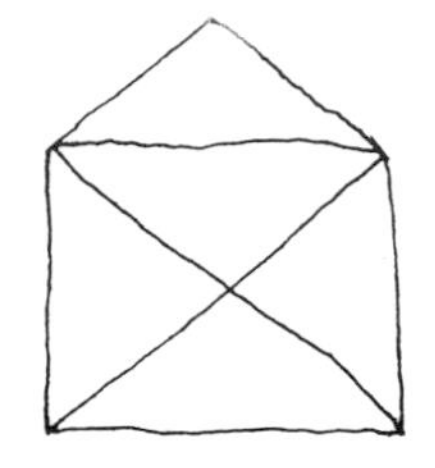

Can you draw this shape without lifting your pencil from the paper? And without retracing any line? When you've figured it out, get some chalk and find a playground.

Ask a friend to try it.

Then have a contest to see who can invent the most shapes that can be drawn without retracing any line and without lifting the chalk. Keep score. Winner gets a milkshake. Everyone else has to clean up the chalk.

This game is topological. (Remember topology?) And there is more to it. You can predict just by looking at a chalk shape (or any other for that matter) whether it can be drawn without lifting the chalk or retracing a line. Topologists tell by looking at the places where lines meet *(vertices)*, and seeing how many of them have an odd number of lines meeting there *(odd vertices)*. Study this chart. The topologists' secret method is lurking here somewhere. Can you tell how they do it? If you're not sure, draw some other figures.

You can do the same thing with letters of the alphabet. Try it.

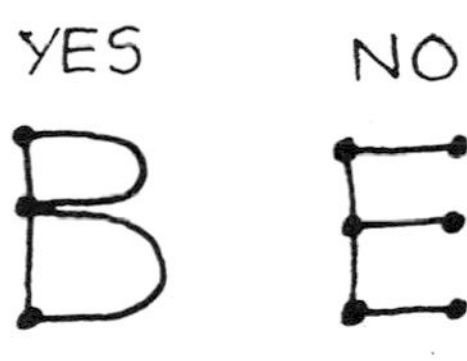

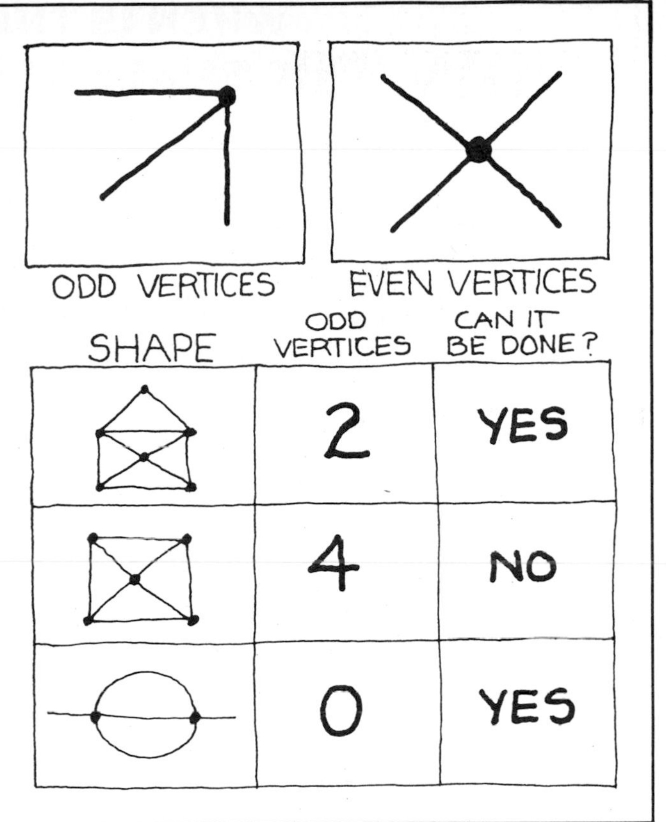

SHAPE	ODD VERTICES	CAN IT BE DONE?
	2	YES
	4	NO
	0	YES

THE RUBBER BALL RIDDLE
or
AN EXERCISE IN LOGICAL THINKING

The best time to try this riddle is when you're outdoors with a tennis ball and plenty of space. It's especially good if your victim is a smart aleck.

Can you throw a ball with all your might and make it stop and come straight back to you without hitting a wall, or the ground, or any other obstruction, and without having anything attached to it?

Moral: The bigger they are, the harder they fall.

WHEN IS THE LETTER O THE SAME AS THE LETTER D?

When they are being looked at by a topologist. Any figures that can be twisted or stretched or squished to make the same shape are topologically the same.

You'll need someone's grandfather for this. It is topologically possible to remove the waistcoat without taking off the jacket. (But be careful, grandfathers are brittle!)

TOPOLOGICAL AMAZEMENTS

Mazes are another preoccupation of topologists. But they are interested not just in getting out of the maze, but also telling whether or not it's *possible* to get out. Sometimes it isn't. Is it possible to get out of both these mazes?

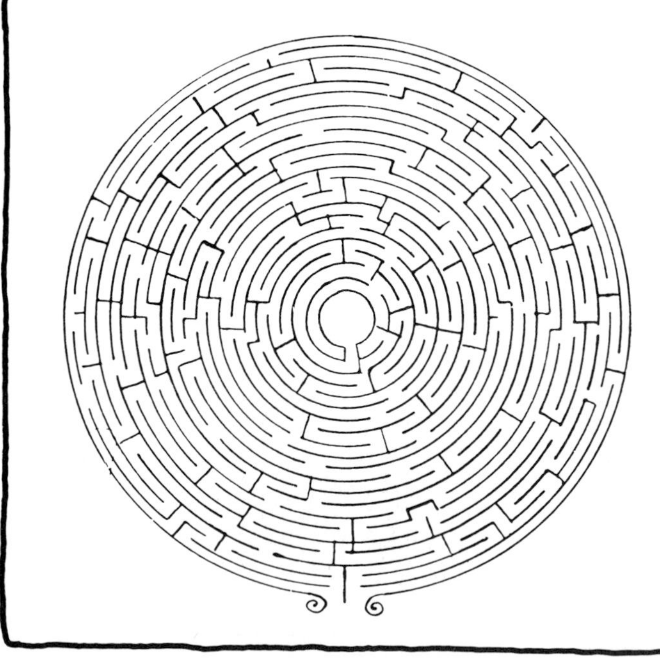

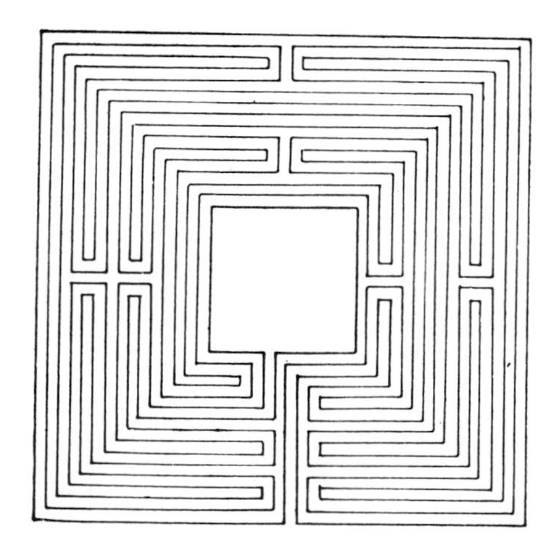

Maybe Grownups Aren't As Smart As You Think

If you don't learn anything else from this book,
it won't matter too much — if you remember
that *grownups don't always know as much as you think they know.*
Especially about mathematics.

Here are some ideas that might help you with
grownups who don't really listen,
or grownups who make you feel
like a dummy.

They'll also be fun to try with grownups
who like to learn new things.

This time, *you* be the teacher.

DOING DISHES

Here is how to get rich in 30 days:

Make an offer to do the dishes (or some other crummy job that grown-ups don't like). Tell them you'll charge 1p the first day, and each day you'll charge twice as much as the day before.

Sounds like a terrible deal, huh? Well, figure out how much you'd earn in 2 weeks. And then in a month. If the grownup that hires you can still afford you by then, you can hire your own dishwasher and take us all on holiday for 2 weeks.

You probably won't get away with this for very long. But it is a very good way to make a point about something called *exponential growth*. And you can bet the next time you make an offer, they'll listen hard!

fathead
FIRST GET A LENGTH OF STRING THAT'S ABOUT 2 METRES LONG. THEN FIND YOURSELF A GROWNUP. ASK IT:
Hey You! How many times do you think this string would have to go around your head to be as long as your body?
(YOU MAY HAVE TO ASK THE QUESTION A COUPLE OF TIMES. BE PATIENT.)
BET YOU A DOUGHNUT THE GROWNUP WILL GUESS WRONG. MATTER OF FACT, YOU MIGHT BET THE GROWNUP A DOUGHNUT. IT'S A SURE DOUGHNUT.
WHAT DOES ALL THIS HAVE TO DO WITH MATHEMATICS? WELL, IT HAS TO DO WITH RATIO, WHICH IS A WAY OF LOOKING AT DIFFERENT ASPECTS OF THE SAME OBJECT.
IS THE RATIO OF YOUR HEAD TO HEIGHT THE SAME AS A GROWNUP'S? MEASURE AND SEE. GUESSING ABOUT HOW ONE THING COMPARES WITH ANOTHER IS SOMETHING WE ALL DO EVERY DAY. BUT WE'RE NOT SO USED TO COMPARING CIRCLES WITH STRAIGHT LINES. SO DON'T BE TOO HARD ON THE GROWNUP.

MORE BODY MATHS

CUT A PIECE OF STRING AS LONG AS YOU ARE TALL. COMPARE THE LENGTH WITH YOUR REACH. ARE YOU A SQUARE? OR A RECTANGLE?

USE THE STRING TO FIND OTHER RATIOS. IS TWICE AROUND YOUR WRIST THE SAME AS ONCE AROUND YOUR NECK? IS YOUR FOOT AS LONG AS ONCE AROUND YOUR WRIST?

THE POPCORN KID ASKS:
IF YOU LINED UP A MILLION PIECES OF POPCORN HOW FAR WOULD IT REACH?
WOULD IT REACH TO THE CORNER?
WOULD IT REACH ANYWHERE?

(MUNCH MUNCH)

This is called "Forehead Knocker" because that's what your grownup will do (knock their forehead) after they have tried this and failed. And they will, unless you happen to have chosen a very clever adult, or a mathematician.

1	2	3	4	5	6	7	8	9	10
★									11
									12
									13
									14

Copy this drawing. Be sure yours has the same number of squares on each side. Make it 10x10. Then sidle up to your grownup.

Say:

"See this drawing? It is a 10x10 grid. Can you figure out, without counting, what number would land in the square with the star if I continued the numbers around?"

After the grownup guesses, count it out. The number is 36 and very few people guess that. Usually the adult will slap its forehead when you tell it. Give it another chance. Say:

"Where would 50 land? How about 100?"

Count them out. Say:

"Does the square where 50 lands look like halfway? Isn't that interesting?"

(And don't look smug. You might not have done any better without this book.)

MORE RATIO STUFF

Check the wastebaskets.

What you need is the paper tube from inside a roll of toilet paper. When you find it, mark it like this:

Then get some string. A piece about 30 centimetres or so will do.

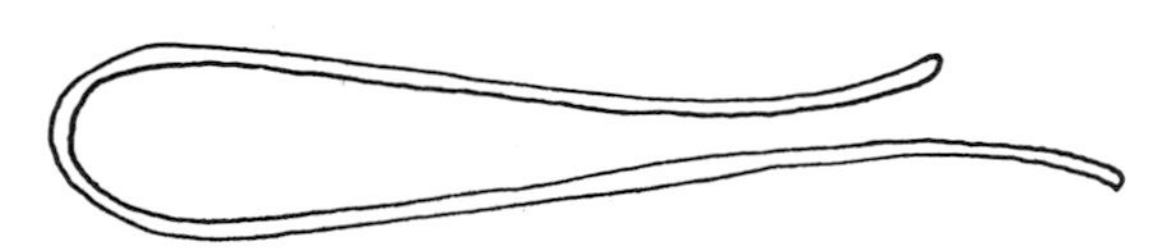

Measure around the tube and cut a piece of string that length. Now guess. If you stretch the string out along the tube, which line is closest to where you think the string will reach? How about that?

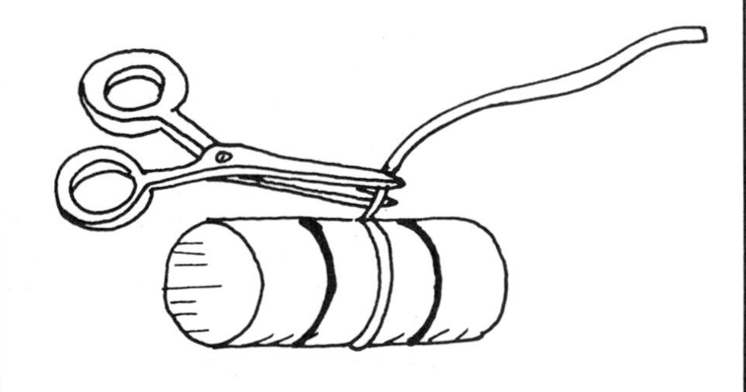

Estimating circular distances is something we're not very used to. The distance around a circular shape *(circumference)* is equal to about 3 times its distance across *(diameter)*. Now that you know that, does it help?

Try it again with some other shapes.

Bet you a grownup doesn't get it either!

WHAT'S NEXT?

Ask a grownup to help you with this number experiment. Be real polite.

Come prepared with a piece of paper and a pencil. If your grownup hesitates, explain that it won't take long. The experiment only involves writing 7 numbers. No adding, subtracting — none of that kind of stuff.

Here are the directions:

You read these numbers and the grownup writes the next larger one each time. That's all there is to it. If you say 14, the grownup writes 15.

Try it. Make sure you read the numbers like this:

"One hundred sixty-three; one thousand, one hundred ninety-four; four hundred thirty-eight; three thousand ninety-nine . . ."

When it's done, look at the last number the grownup wrote on the paper. If it's 4000, show the adult what you read.

you say.

If it's 3100, then the grownup is no mathematical dummy and you had better remember that person the next time you need help with your maths homework.

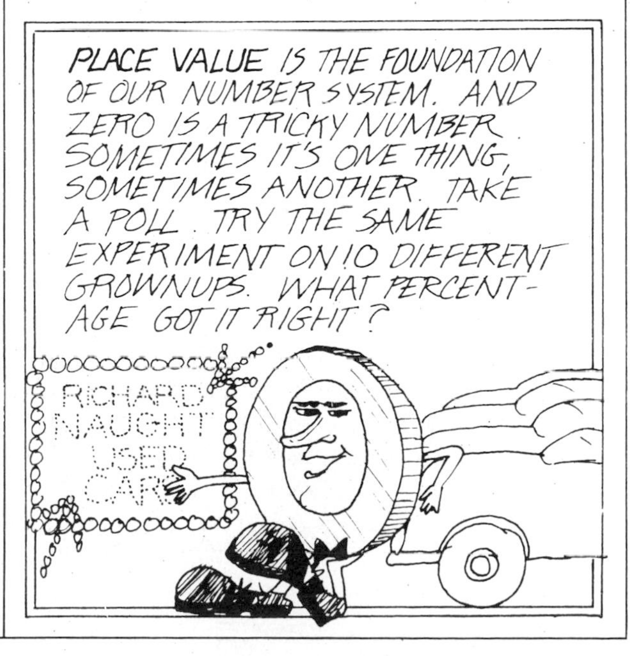

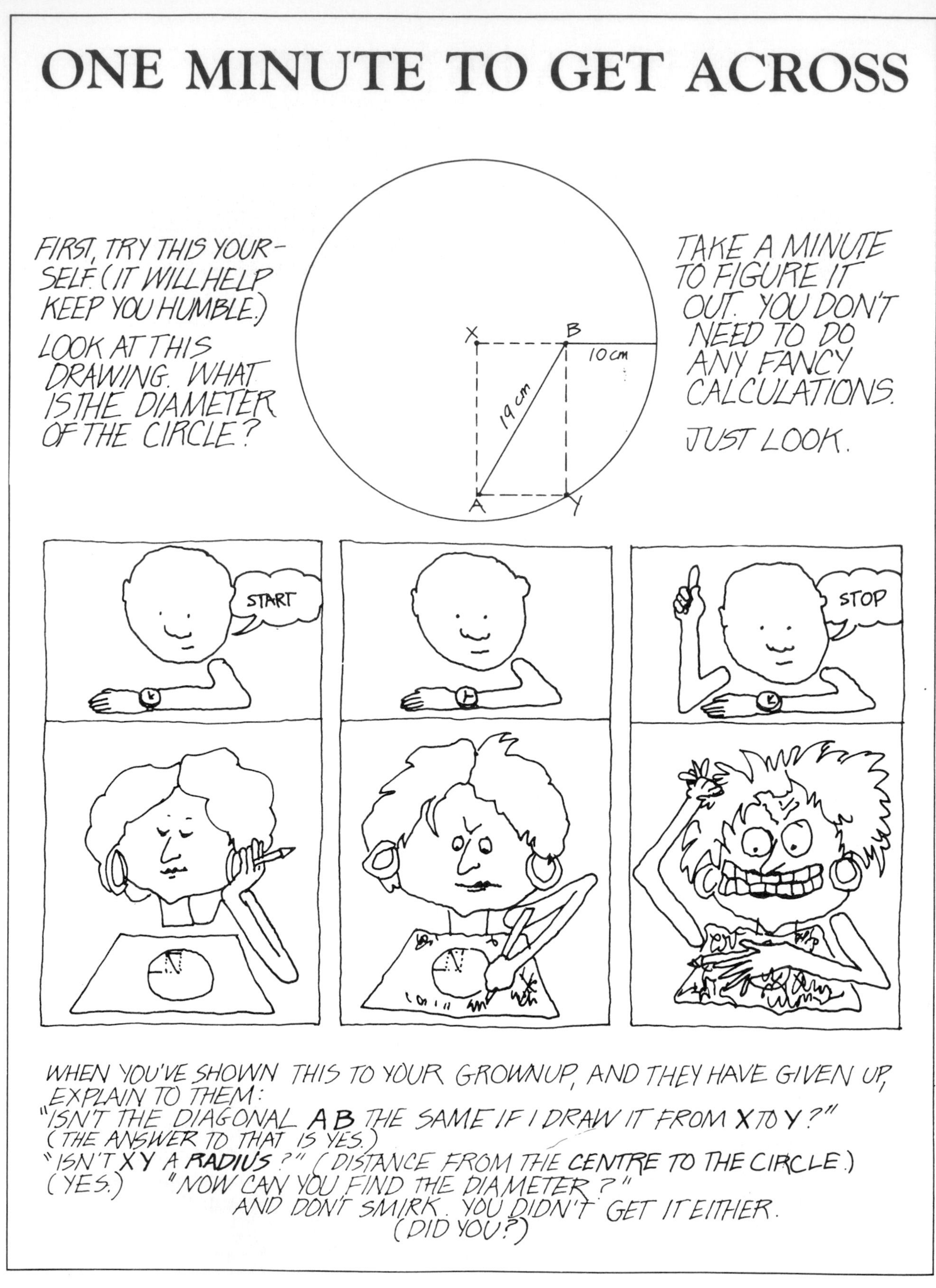
ONE MINUTE TO GET ACROSS
FIRST, TRY THIS YOURSELF. (IT WILL HELP KEEP YOU HUMBLE.)
LOOK AT THIS DRAWING. WHAT IS THE DIAMETER OF THE CIRCLE?
X
B
10 cm
19 cm
A
Y
TAKE A MINUTE TO FIGURE IT OUT. YOU DON'T NEED TO DO ANY FANCY CALCULATIONS.
JUST LOOK.
START
STOP
WHEN YOU'VE SHOWN THIS TO YOUR GROWNUP, AND THEY HAVE GIVEN UP, EXPLAIN TO THEM:
"ISN'T THE DIAGONAL AB THE SAME IF I DRAW IT FROM X TO Y?"
(THE ANSWER TO THAT IS YES.)
"ISN'T XY A RADIUS?" (DISTANCE FROM THE CENTRE TO THE CIRCLE.)
(YES.) "NOW CAN YOU FIND THE DIAMETER?"
AND DON'T SMIRK. YOU DIDN'T GET IT EITHER.
(DID YOU?)

The Rabbit and the Mathematicians

Once upon a time there was a rabbit and 2 mathematicians. They all knew a problem when they saw one. The rabbit was in a hole. He had the problem. One of the mathematicians sat under a tree and said:

"If the rabbit can jump halfway to the top of the hole each time it takes a leap, it will never get to the top because no matter how close it gets, it will only get halfway."

The other mathematician crawled to the edge of the hole and peeked over the side. He said:

"Hmmm. Even though theoretically speaking the rabbit only goes halfway each time, when it gets close enough to the top, it will just scramble over the edge and be out!"

WILL THE RABBIT GET OUT OF THE HOLE?
WHICH MATHEMATICIAN IS CORRECT?

P.S. Mathematicians who sit under trees and think about things and don't worry too much about solutions are called *theoretical mathematicians.* The kind that crawl to the edges of holes and think about ideas that can be put to use are called *applied mathematicians.* Which kind are you?

rollups

To do this experiment you'll have to get hold of a piece of thick paper (cartridge paper works fine) about 20 cm × 30 cm. Also a pair of scissors, some sticky tape, and a container with rice, lentils, or something dry like that in it. (Borrow it from the kitchen because you can bring it back when you're done.)

Now you have to hook your grownup. Say:

"I've been thinking about volume." (Remember volume? That's the word for how much space something takes up.)

Then cut the paper in half. Be sure you cut in the middle.

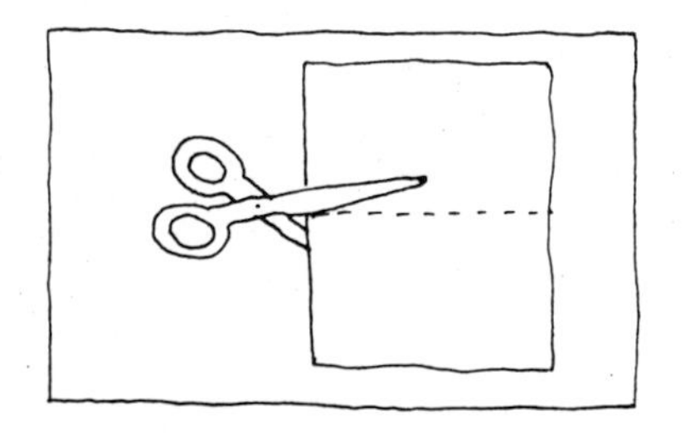

"These 2 pieces have the same *area*, right? (That's the word for how much space a flat surface covers.)

Now roll each paper into a tube. One the long way, the other the short way. Tape the ends.

"Does each tube hold the same amount?"

(What do you think the answer is? Try it first and find out.)

This experiment relates volume to area. Volume is a 3-dimensional measure. Area is a 2-dimensional measure. What difference does that make?

RIDDLES

You can't fool all of them all of the time.

But you can try.

These riddles all have something to do with mathematics. Sort of. They've been around a long time. But even if your grownup remembers hearing them before, chances are they won't remember the answer.

When you ask a riddle you might get answers like this:

WHAT IS THIS? YOUR HOMEWORK?

or:
"What do you want to know for?"
or:
"Go ask your mother."
or:
"Why don't you go outside and play?"

Don't be discouraged. Say:

THIS IS MATHEMATICAL.

Then ask it again.

Two kids were playing **draughts**. They played 5 games and each kid won the same number of games and there were no ties. How can this be?

When the grownup gives up, tell the answer.

They weren't playing each other.

And brace yourself for the grownup's next question:

What does <u>that</u> have to do with mathematics?

Arithmetic is only a part of mathematics. Logical thinking is just as important.

Now <u>you</u> decide whether you should ask this grownup more riddles or move on to another.

MORE RIDDLES

Here are some more riddles. We've put the answers upside down. So try them first yourself. (Maybe this book is doing you some good after all.) Then peek at the answer.

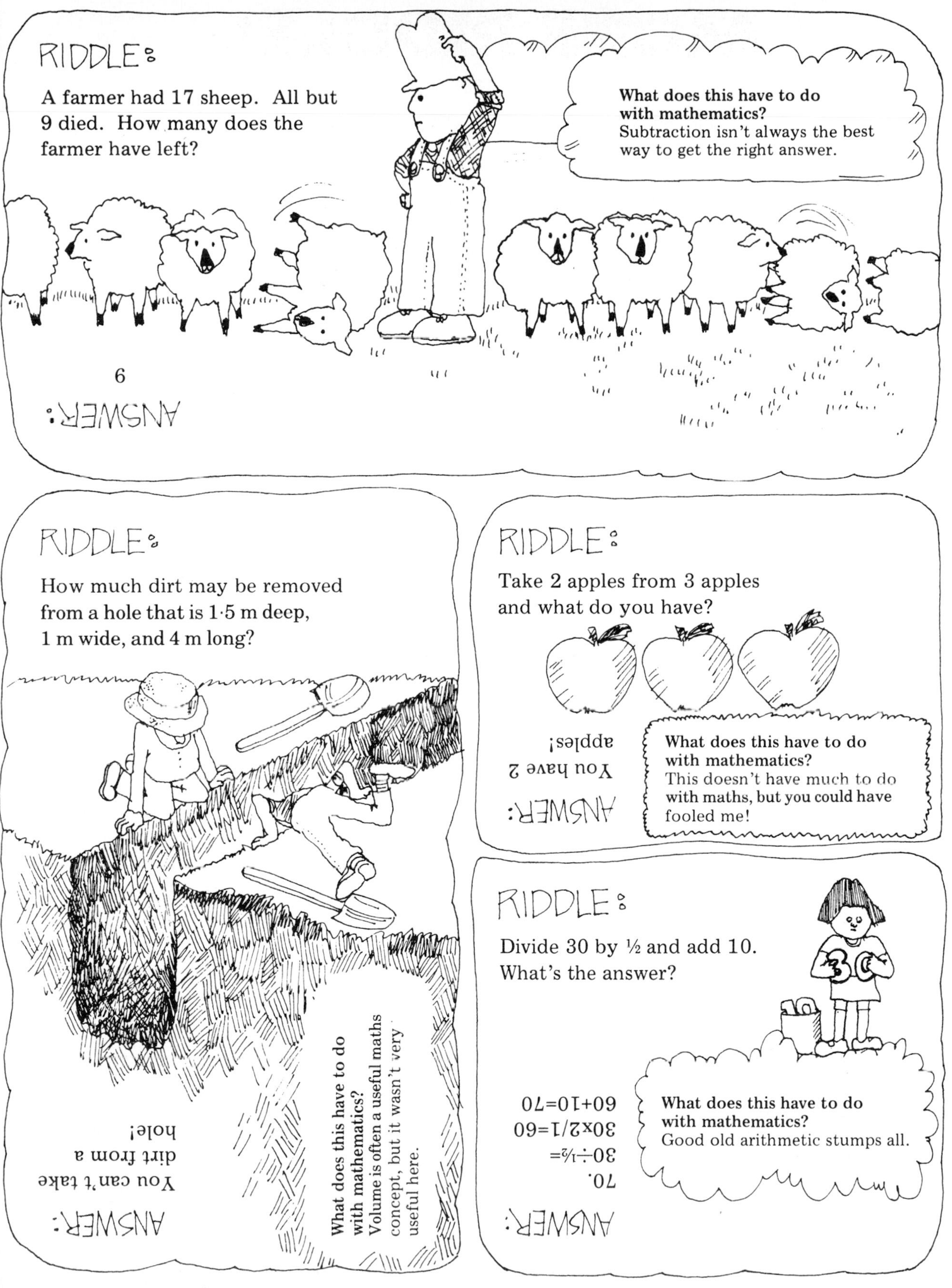
RIDDLE:
A farmer had 17 sheep. All but 9 died. How many does the farmer have left?
What does this have to do with mathematics?
Subtraction isn't always the best way to get the right answer.
ANSWER:
9
RIDDLE:
How much dirt may be removed from a hole that is 1·5 m deep, 1 m wide, and 4 m long?
What does this have to do with mathematics?
Volume is often a useful maths concept, but it wasn't very useful here.
ANSWER:
You can't take dirt from a hole!
RIDDLE:
Take 2 apples from 3 apples and what do you have?
What does this have to do with mathematics?
This doesn't have much to do with maths, but you could have fooled me!
ANSWER:
You have 2 apples!
RIDDLE:
Divide 30 by ½ and add 10. What's the answer?
30
10
What does this have to do with mathematics?
Good old arithmetic stumps all.
ANSWER:
70.
30÷½=
30x2/1=60
60+10=70

RIDDLE:
If your bedroom were pitch dark and you needed a pair of matching socks, how many socks would you need to take out of the drawer if there are 10 white socks and 10 blue ones?
What does this have to do with mathematics? A little probability theory comes in handy here.
ANSWER: 3
RIDDLE:
I've got 2 coins that total 55 pence. One of the coins is not a 5p. What are the 2 coins?
ANSWER: A 50p coin and a 5p. One's not a 5p; the other is.
What does this have to do with mathematics? Logic wins again.
RIDDLE:
If the doctor gave you 3 pills and said to take 1 every ½ hour, how long would they last?
ANSWER: 1 hour.
What does this have to do with mathematics? Measurement is an important part of maths. Time is one area of measurement.
RIDDLE:
There are twelve 1p stamps in a dozen, but how many 2p stamps are there in a dozen?
ANSWER: 12
What does this have to do with mathematics? A dozen is a dozen is a dozen.
RIDDLE:
What's the smallest number of birds that could fly in this formation: 2 birds in front of a bird, 2 birds behind a bird, and a bird between 2 birds?
ANSWER: 3 birds in a row, 1 behind the other.
What does this have to do with mathematics? Geometrical patterns of flight are fascinating.

Things to Do When You Have the Flu

You're in bed because the doctor said you have to rest.
There is no more sleep anywhere in your body.
You're sick of reading.
Your mother won't play draughts and no one else is home.

There is nothing to watch on TV.
And you think you might start to whine any time now.

Try a little mathematical medicine.
Bleh, you say?
It can be taken in bed and doesn't require much equipment.
Pencil, scissors, stuff like that.

It'll make you (mathematically) strong.

TOOTHPICKING

First find 24 toothpicks. Arrange them like this: →

Ready?

How many squares do these toothpicks make? (And don't say 9. Keep looking until you find all 14.)

Take away just 8 toothpicks, so you will have just 2 squares left. (Now this is not your run-of-the-mill subtraction problem. In fact it has more to do with geometry.)

What's the least number of toothpicks you need to build 1 square? Four!

What about 2 squares? Seven?

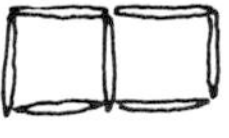

Three squares?
And so on. Can you find a pattern?

TOOTHPICKS	SQUARES
4	1
7	2
	3

Use 12 toothpicks. Place them any way you wish. How many different numbers of squares can you make?

Tired of squares? Try triangles.

Want to build bigger shapes? Use some little balls of modeling clay or some whole dried peas that have soaked until they're soft. You can build magnificent mathematical structures. Cubes. Tetrahedrons.

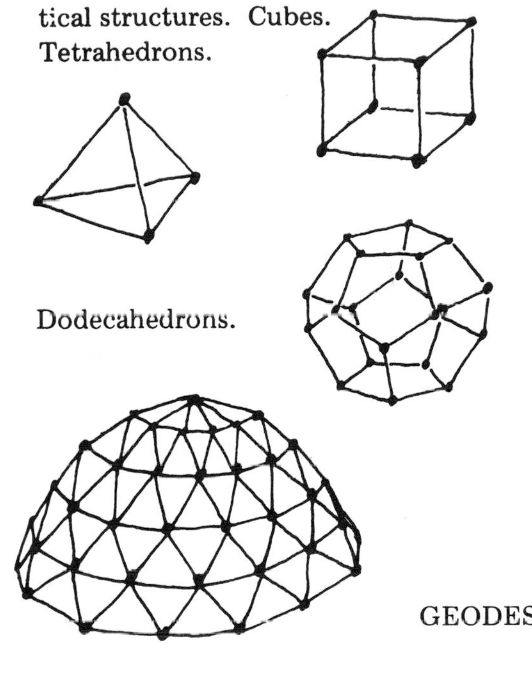

Dodecahedrons.

GEODESICS.

One last toothpick tickler. Can you arrange 6 toothpicks so that each one touches all the others? (It can be done!)

SQUARING UP

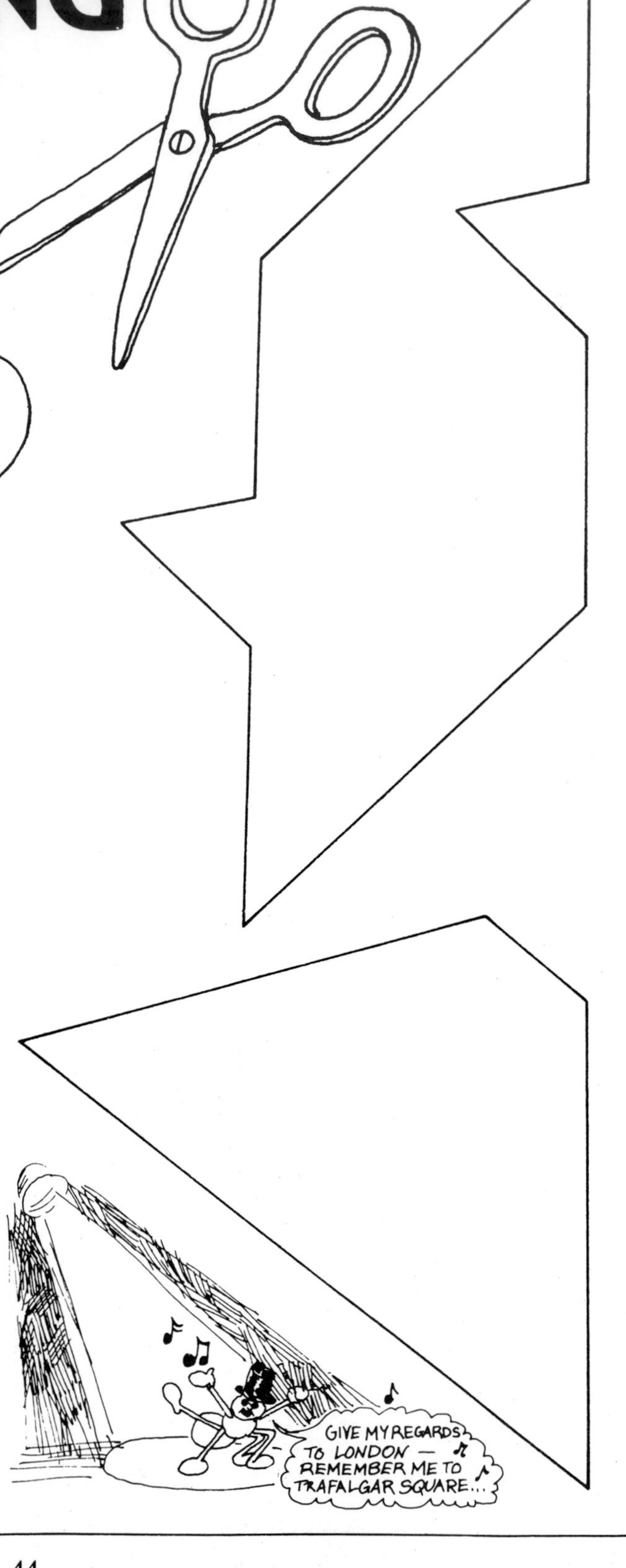

Copy this shape onto a piece of paper.

Then cut it out.

Now, if you copied it carefully, you should be able to make 1 cut somewhere on the shape, then put the 2 pieces together to make a square!

Try it.

If that was too easy, then try these, smarty! One more cut to make a square!

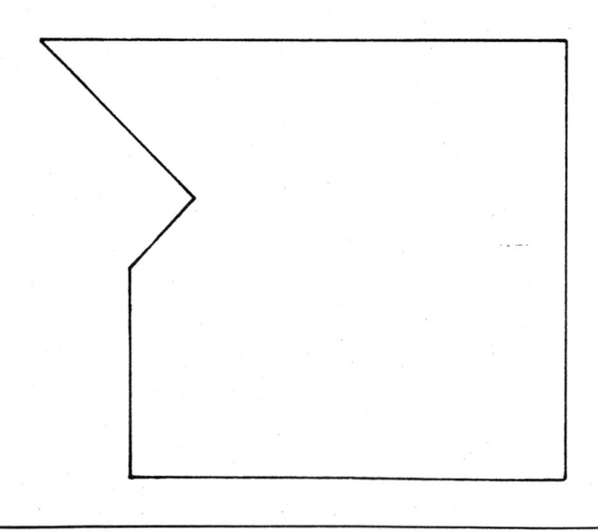

SPEAKING THE LANGUAGE

In case you hadn't noticed already, mathematicians have a language all their own. Fancy words like *topology* and *square root* and *dodecahedron* are all words they have made up to stand for their tools, or other things they work with. Even rounders players have special words, it's just that we're more used to *them*.

Suppose you had never played rounders before and it's your turn to be in, only you aren't sure what to do and someone yells, "Where's the batter?" and all you can think of is raw pancakes. Well, that's how it is with mathematics only most of the words don't sound like *anything* you know about. What should you do?

First, don't worry about it too much. Second, don't expect the word to make any sense at all (or try to remember it), until you've become familiar with whatever the word is about.

And remember, mathematical language is sort of like a code. It's a short way of writing down a mathematical idea. Here are some examples:

English

goin' fishin'
got no bait
eight times six
is forty-eight

Mathematics

the result of
multiplying the
factors 6 and 8
is the product
48.

Code

$6 \times 8 = 48$

the perfect palindrome
OHHO!
I'M A PALINDROME. A REGULAR KIND OF NUMBER. IT DOESN'T MATTER HOW YOU APPROACH ME. FRONTWARDS OR BACKWARDS I LOOK THE SAME. I CAN BE ANY SIZE YOU LIKE. I CAN TURN UP ANYWHERE.....IN YOUR HOUSE NUMBERS, CAR NUMBER PLATES, TELEPHONE NUMBERS.
YOU CAN GET TO ME WITH A BIT OF ADDITION. TAKE 137 FOR INSTANCE. IT'S NOT A PALINDROME, BUT REVERSE IT AND ADD. SHAZAM!
137
+731
868
A PALINDROME!

SOMETIMES IT TAKES A LITTLE LONGER TO GET ME. LIKE 68, FOR EXAMPLE.....
68
+86
154
+451
605
+506
1111
THERE, YOU SEE!
AND SOME NUMBERS TAKE MUCH LONGER TO REACH ME. TRY 89......BUT BE SURE YOU HAVE A LOT OF PAPER.
THERE ARE WORD PALINDROMES TOO. LIKE WOW! DAD! RADAR! AND SENTENCE PALINDROMES LIKE:
TOO HOT TO HOOT.
NO LEMONS, NO MELON.
TEN ANIMALS I SLAM IN A NET.
What will be the next YEAR that is also a PALINDROME?

You need some thick paper. (Or thin card.) And scissors.

Cut 5 squares like this one from thick paper.

Arrange them in different ways. Their edges must be touching. And their corners must be lined up.

This is okay.

This is not okay.

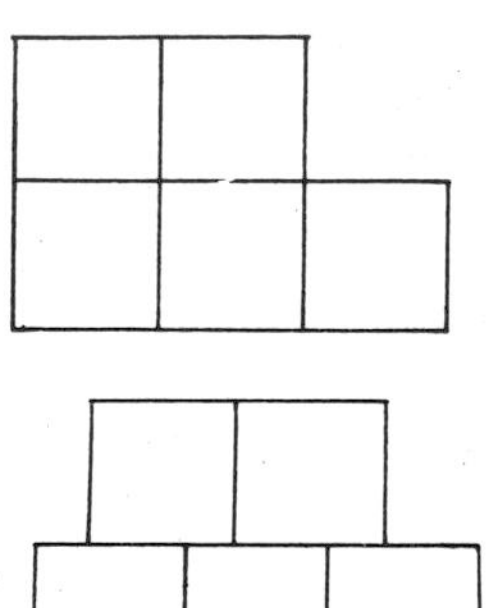

You think there are lots of ways to do that? There are 12. Can you find all 12? Draw them as you do. A rule to follow as you search: if a shape could be cut out and fit exactly over another shape, it doesn't count as different.

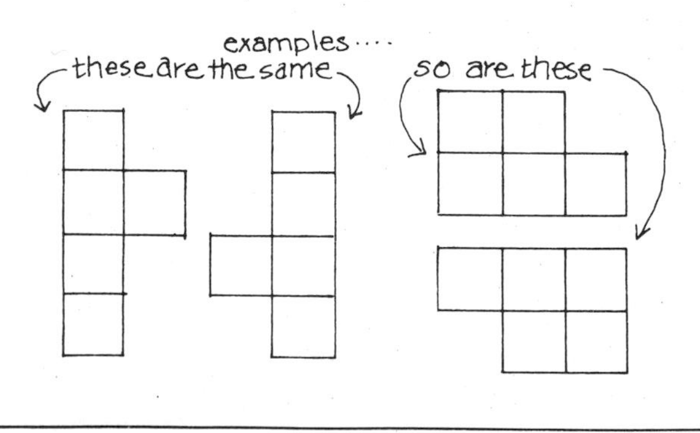

You have been looking for *pentominoes*.

Look at these 2 pentominoes. This one would fold up into a box. X marks the bottom of the box.

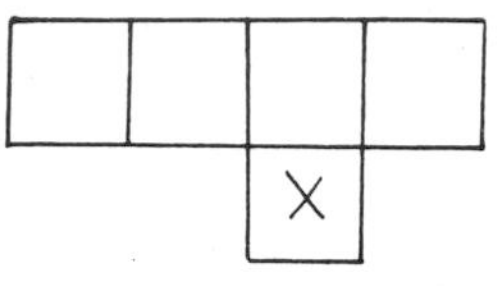

This one wouldn't fold up into a box.

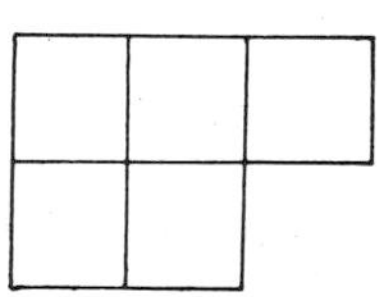

Now look at the pentominoes you drew. If you drew all 12, 8 of them should fold up into boxes. Find them and mark the bottoms. Then cut them out and fold them to see if you are right.

Now you're ready for

THE FACTORY BOX PROBLEM

A factory needs topless boxes. Like this.

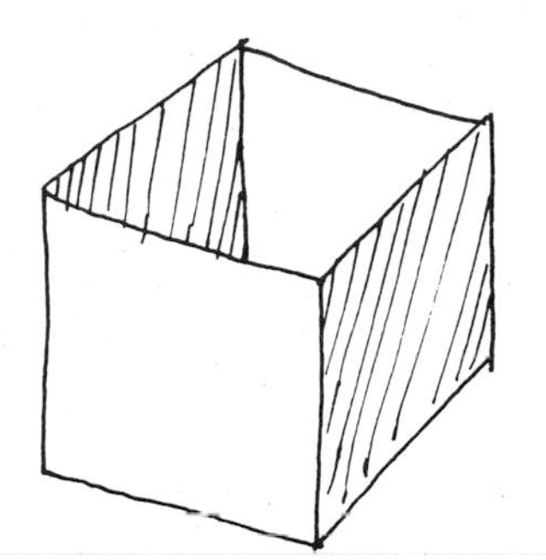

Someone in the ordering department bought a whole lot of cardboard, like this.

Each box will take 5 squares.

Since there are 20 squares on the sheet, they should be able to get 4 topless boxes out of each big sheet.

Will they?

How would you cut the cardboard?

NOT MORE BOXES!?

Yes!

If you had a piece of paper like this,

and you cut a square the same size from each corner like this,

you could fold up what's left to make a box. Right?

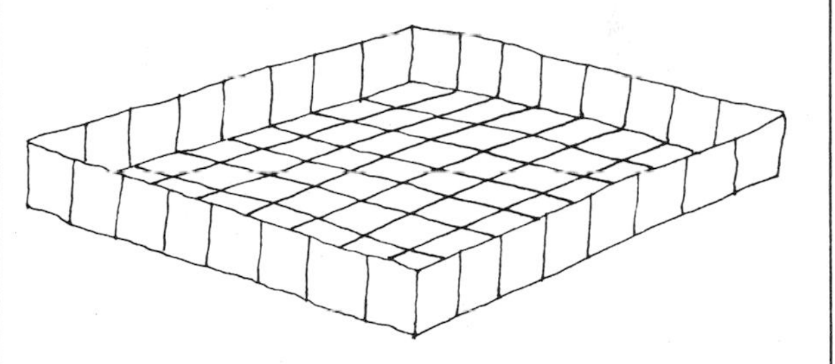

What size square would you cut out of each corner to make the box that would hold the most?

This is an experiment that connects the volume of a box with its *surface area* (how much space its outside would cover).

prime
I'm PRIME! I belong to a class of numbers that has a special characteristic.
Pick a number, like 12.
If you had 12 squares of paper and you were going to arrange them in a rectangle, you'd have several choices.
Too many choices.
12 is not prime.
What if you picked a number like 7.
If you had 7 squares, there's only 1 shape rectangle you could make. Only 1 shape;
7 IS PRIME!
A number either is or is not prime.
Try 6.
Nope.
Try 5.
Yes, prime.
16? 2?
10?
9?
21? 11?
7

Mathematicians try to find patterns to predict when we prime numbers will appear. They have a fancy way to describe us:
A PRIME NUMBER HAS ONLY 2 FACTORS: ITSELF AND 1.
(which means there are only 2 numbers which divide into a prime number exactly).
But we primes are not very obvious. Here are the first few prime numbers: 2, 3, 5, 7, 11, 13, 17, . . .
1 2 3 4 5 6 7 8 9 10 11
If you're interested, colour in the primes on a chart like this. — it's the closest to a pattern you can find.
1 2 3 4 5 6
7 8 9 10 11 12
13 14 15 16 17 18
19 20 21 22 23 24
25 26 27 28 29 30
You may have wondered why 1 isn't prime. Well, it just isn't. Those mathematicians get awfully picky sometimes.
Goldbach was a mathematician who made a CONJECTURE. He said that every even number can be written as the sum of 2 prime numbers. (16 = 11+5, 30 = 17+13, etc.)
No one has ever proved it. But no one has ever disproved it either. That's why it's called a CONJECTURE.

WHO NEEDS A CEILING? or Dots Enough!

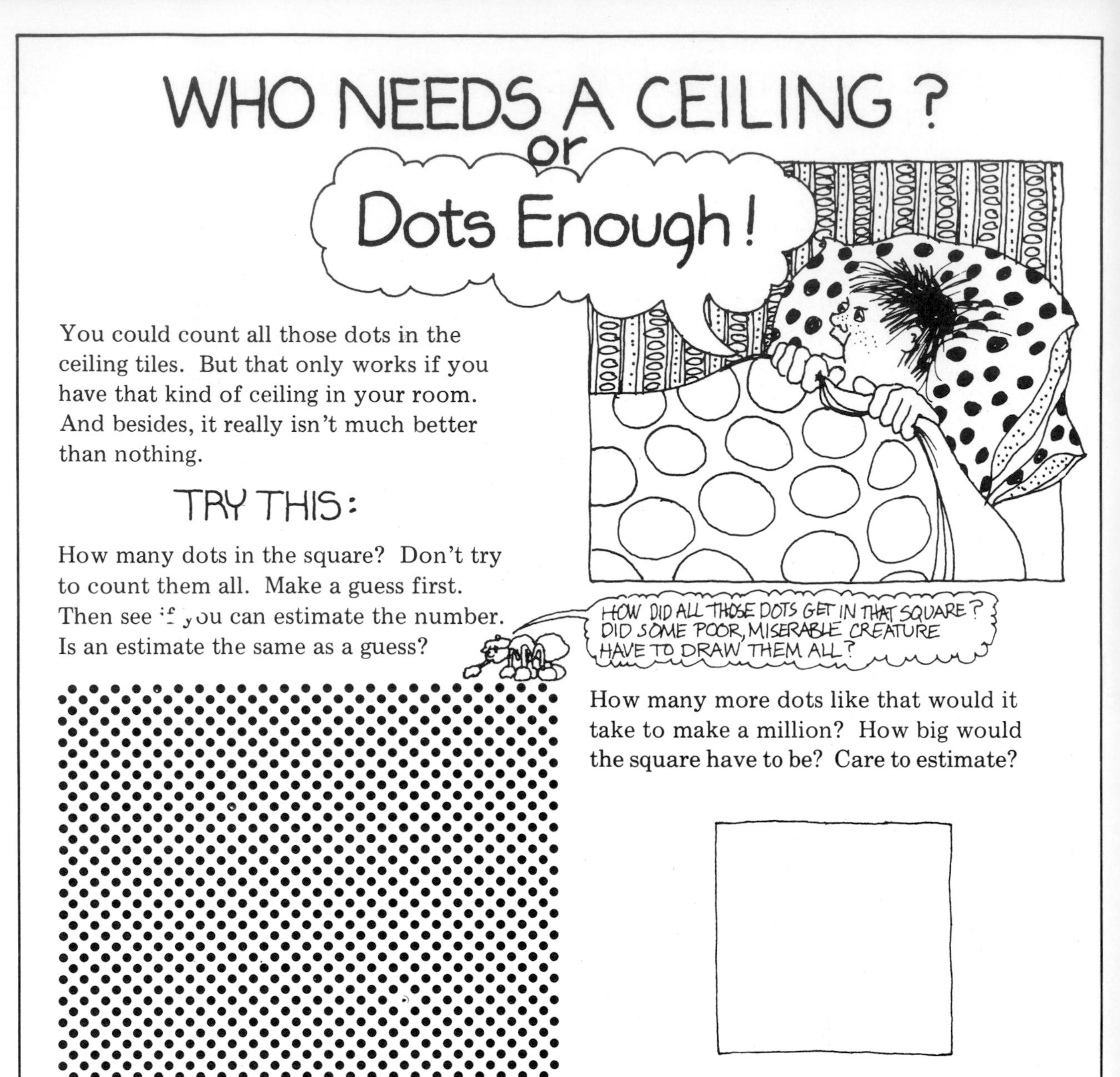

You could count all those dots in the ceiling tiles. But that only works if you have that kind of ceiling in your room. And besides, it really isn't much better than nothing.

TRY THIS:

How many dots in the square? Don't try to count them all. Make a guess first. Then see if you can estimate the number. Is an estimate the same as a guess?

How many more dots like that would it take to make a million? How big would the square have to be? Care to estimate?

Here is another square. How many dots do you think you could put in a square this size if you were willing to make dots until it was full?

On the next page are some dot-pictures. If the dots were all very tiny, the pictures would look just like in a newspaper. Put the book at the end of your bed and squint at it. That's how photographs get printed. How many dots in the banana? In the pie?

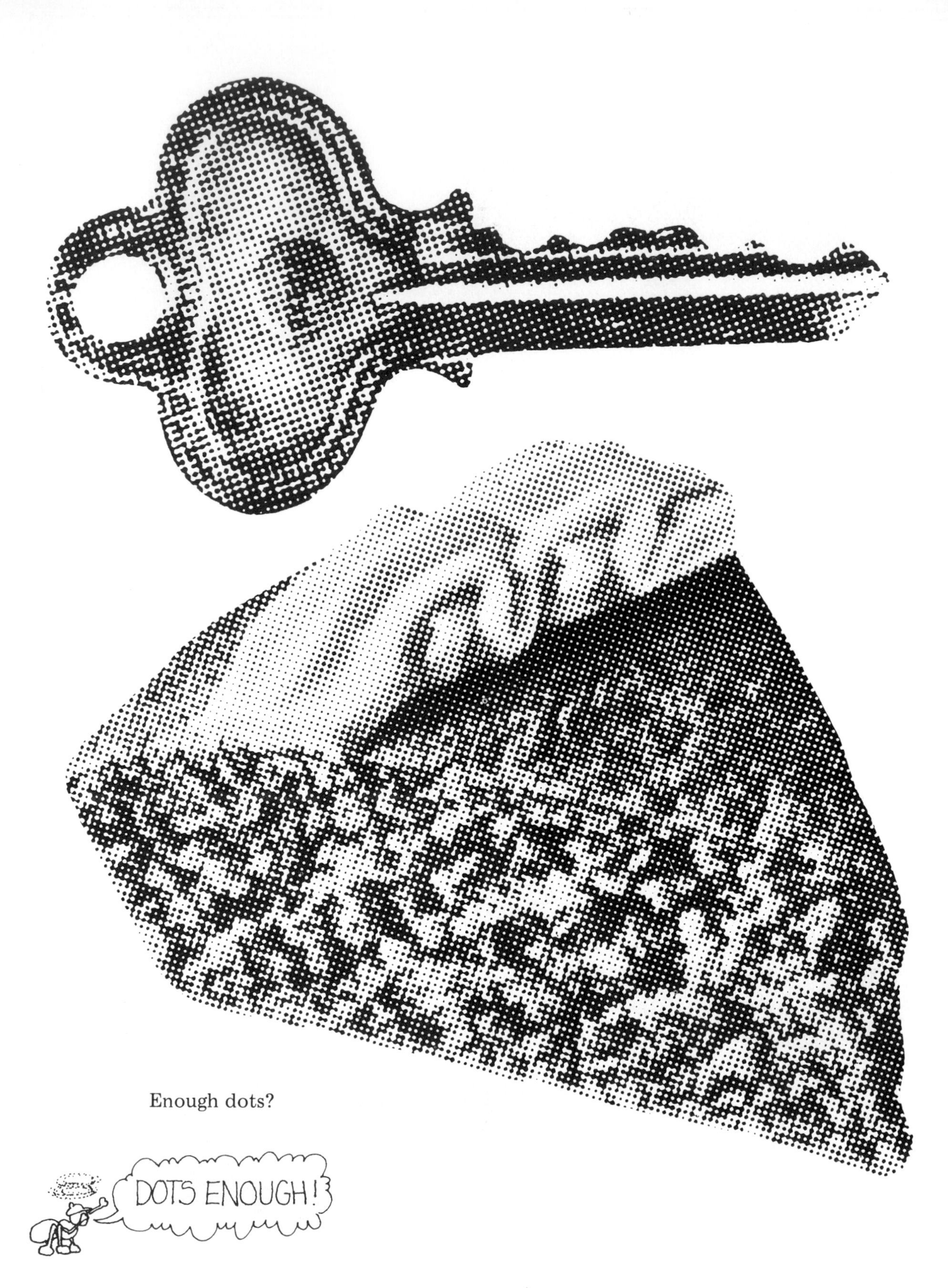

Enough dots?

A Mathe-magic Show

Some people think that *everything* mathematical is magic.

(What they don't know won't hurt them.)

THE EMBRACING PAPERCLIPS
•TAKE A COMMON STRIP OF WRITING PAPER.
•CURVE IT SO IT MATCHES THIS DRAWING
•CLIP THE PAPER CLIPS TO IT SO THAT THEY LOOK EXACTLY LIKE THIS
NOW HAVE YOUR ASSISTANT HOLD THE ENDS OF THE PAPER THUS:
THEN YOU SAY THE MAGIC WORDS:
RAN*DA*DAN*DA*DAN*DANDY!
AND WHEN YOUR ASSISTANT PULLS THE ENDS OF THE PAPER HARD,
THOSE HUMDRUM, COMMON PAPER CLIPS WILL FLY OFF THE PAPER,
AND LEAP INTO EACH OTHER'S ARMS!

MATHEMATICALLY, THIS FEAT HAS SOMETHING TO DO WITH THE CURVE IN THE PAPER GETTING TRANSFERRED TO THE CLIPS— ONE OF THOSE PHENOMENA TOPOLOGISTS LOOK AT. (REMEMBER TOPOLOGY?)

IT WILL ALSO WORK WITH A £5 NOTE. BORROW ONE FROM SOMEONE IN YOUR AUDIENCE. (MAYBE THEY WILL BE SO STUNNED BY YOUR BRILLIANCE THEY WILL FORGET TO ASK FOR IT BACK.)

SMART CARDS

First you need to make 5 smart cards like these. Number them exactly as they are here. Make them big enough so your audience can see the numbers clearly.

Ask someone to pick any number between 1 and 31. Then they need to point to *each* card in which their number appears.

Then you will tell them what number they picked. How will you know? Try it yourself. Choose a number. Find it in the cards shown here.

Now add up the first number of each card that your number appears in. The total is the number you picked. Right?

Binary is a word which has to do with the number **2**. Look at the first number in each box: **1, 2, 4, 8, 16**. They are all powers of **2**. Which is another way of saying that you multiply each one by **2** to get the next one.

So these are very smart cards.

Once you know the system, you can't miss.

If it didn't work, try it again. The magic in this trick is because of something called the *binary system* which is also what all computers are based on. If it didn't work, either you're wrong, or all the computers in the world are wrong. So try again.

The old "Which Hand" trick

Tell a person from the audience to put a 10p coin in one hand and a penny in the other. The person should be able to add or multiply without resorting to a piece of paper and pencil. So try it on some smart adult. In this trick you can figure out which coin is in which hand.

You say:

"Put one coin in your left hand, and the other in your right. You can show the audience, but don't tell me."

"Now, multiply what's in your right hand by 4, 6, or 8. (Give them a little time.) Got it? Don't give me the number."

"Now multiply what's in your left hand by 3, 5, or 7. Okay?"

"Now add those answers up. And give me the total."

Now you tell which hand is holding which coin. If the total is even, the penny is in the *right* hand. If the total is odd, the penny is in the *left* hand.

Thanks to something mathematicians refer to as *place value*, this trick will never fail, unless, of course, your smart adult turns out to be a dummy. Place value has to do with 1's and 10's (and where you put decimal points). The number in the 1's place tells us whether a number is even or odd. See if you can tell how this trick works.

If, by some chance, *no one* in your audience has a 10p coin, and you're stuck with a 5p and a penny, here is a sneaky way to go ahead and do the trick anyway without damaging your reputation as a magician. When you get to the part where they multiply, just say:

"Multiply what's in your right hand by 14. Okay? Now multiply what's in your left hand by 14. Got it? Add them together and tell me the total."

Now multiplying a penny by 14 is simple. Right? But multiplying *5p* by 14 will set most people looking for paper and pencil. Watch their face. You'll know which hand the 5p is in!
(The adding part is just to throw them off.)

Sneaky, huh?

SLIDING IN

You've got to try this! The object is to move the 5p coin without touching it.

Put the penny in between the 2p and the 5p. You may move only one coin, and it can't be the 5p.

Ready?

Put your right index finger on the 2p. Slide it to the right and then slide it back quickly so it hits the penny — hard.

You didn't move the 5p, did you? Magic did!

A blend of logical argument and Newton's second law of motion explains this one.

How far can you make the 5p slide using this method? Experiment and see. Would the 5p slide farther if you used a 10p coin instead of a 2p? What if all three were 5p coins? Can you find the maximum distance a coin can be moved like this?

THE STUPENDOUS COLOSSAL "WHAT'S LEFT" CARD TRICK

This is an incredible trick that will leave your audience breathless and amazed. If they knew how you did it, it would leave them mean and angry because it is really a huge put-on! But it is based on very clear and logical thinking — something most people forget about when they *think* they are watching magic!

Someone will pick a card. You will find it in the deck behind your back without looking. You can't believe it? Just wait!

You need 1 deck of playing cards. Shuffle them and do all those things people do with cards so you don't look suspicious to the audience. Actually, none of that matters. While you are shuffling, glance at the bottom card. Then put the deck face down. It won't be touched again until the very end of the trick.

Remember the bottom card. Everything depends on it.

Now. What is going to happen is that during the course of this trick, your audience will choose a card. And it will be the card on the bottom of the deck. So there will be no problem finding it!

Suppose the bottom card is the 5 of clubs. You have to get them to pick *that* card. This is how you do it. Start with the clubs part. Here's what to say:

1. *Name the 4 suits.* (Listen, if you've got a card-ignorant audience, you might as well forget the trick. They won't be impressed anyway.)

2. *Pick 2 of them.* (Suppose they say, "Hearts and diamonds?" Gulp, you think. Don't worry. What's the title of this trick? "What's Left." That's the secret. You don't like what they pick, you just say, "What's left?" Okay?)

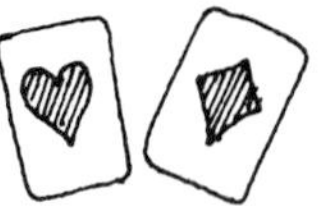

3. *What's left?* ("Clubs and spades," they say.)

4. *Now pick 1 of them.* (If they pick spades just ask, "What's left?" If they pick clubs, just say:)

5. *Good! Let's remember clubs.* (Don't sound too relieved or they might catch on!)

That takes care of the clubs part.

6. *Now, what are the numbers and face cards in each suit, starting with ace?*

7. *Pick 4 of them. Name them in order.* (Suppose they say, "Ten, jack, queen, king." That won't do at all. So just ask:)

8. *What's left?* (They'll probably look at you in horror, but if they picked 4 in order like you suggested, it won't be too bad. Be patient with them.)

Now keep doing this until they pick 4 cards that include the 5, like 3, 4, 5, 6. Then say:

9. *Pick 2.* (5 and 6)

10. *Pick 1.* (6)

11. *What's left?* (5) Aha!

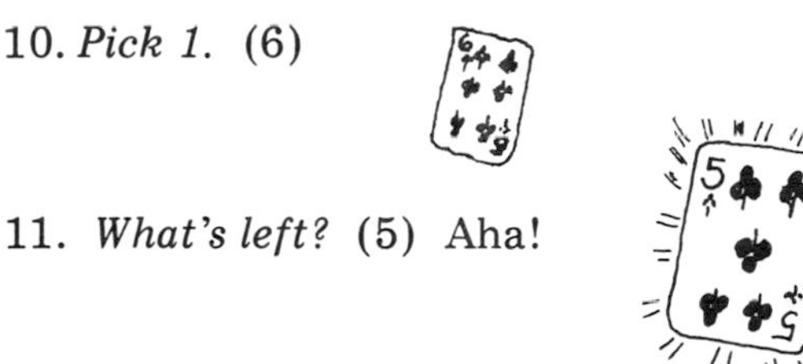

12. *Okay. Five. And what suit did you pick?* (Clubs.)

Now for the finale . . . Pick up the deck and hold it behind your back. Do not even glance at it. Say:

It really doesn't matter, does it? Take your time. Pretend to concentrate *very* hard. If they give you 3 chances (usually they will give you more than 1), you might miss the first one.

Take your time.

They don't believe you can do it anyway.

Little do they know!

THE FAMOUS ANSWER-BEFORE-THE-QUESTION TRICK
This is not a trick for the faint-hearted. If there are any in your audience who can't tolerate the shock of a truly astounding experience, you had better ask them to leave the room now.
For in this trick you will
GIVE THE ANSWER BEFORE THE QUESTION!
(And it will be the right answer.)
Concentrate very hard. Write the number 1,089 on a piece of paper.
Show it to 1 person, then ask them to keep it, but not to reveal what the answer is.
Say in a grand voice:
There is the answer. Now I need a question.
Choose someone else from the audience.
Ask them to give you a number with 3 different digits, but make sure that the first and third digits have a difference of more than one.
287
Next ask them to reverse the digits and subtract 1 3-digit number from the other.
782
-287
495

Reverse that answer and add it to the first answer.
594
+495
1089
The total will always be 1089! (If you subtract and add correctly.)
!
!
Ask your 2 subjects to compare answers and then tell the audience ....
1089
....BUT DON'T TELL HOW YOU DID THE TRICK. IF YOUR AUDIENCE IS STUMPED AND YOU HAVE TO DO IT AGAIN, THERE'S A GOOD CHANCE *THEY* WILL BEGIN TO SEE THE PATTERN. SO ONLY DO THAT TRICK ONCE!
BE SURE TO PICK PEOPLE WHO CAN ADD AND SUBTRACT!
I CAN'T FIGURE IT OUT!
NO!
HOW CAN THIS BE!
I DON'T BELIEVE IT!
WELL I GOTTA BE GOING...

THE RUBBER BAND THAT LISTENS

(It's really a plain old rubber band, but you will make it appear to do exactly what you want.)

Hold up the rubber band. Say:

Then you should have some hocus-pocus build-up and at the right moment tell the rubber band to jump from your first 2 fingers to your last 2.

What the audience sees:

The rubber band moves from

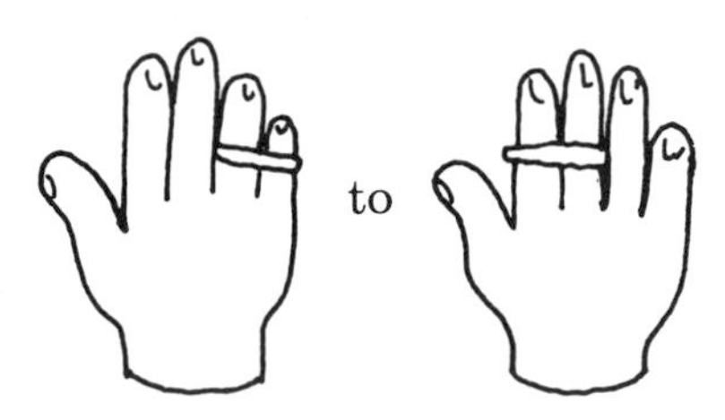

It takes a little practice to do it smoothly. Here's how it works:

Put the band around your 3rd and 4th fingers.

Pull it out so everyone can see.

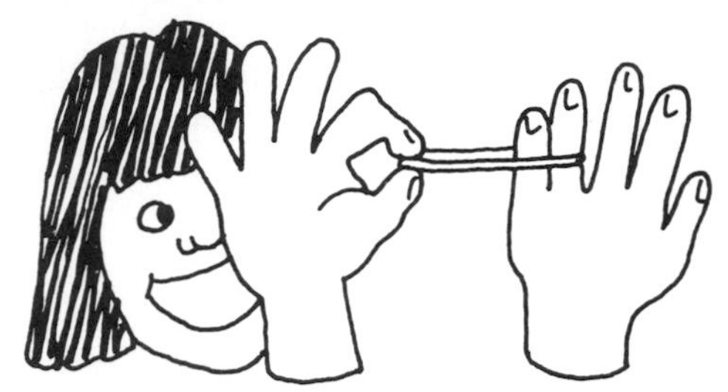

Turn your palm out and pull it again so they can see the other side.

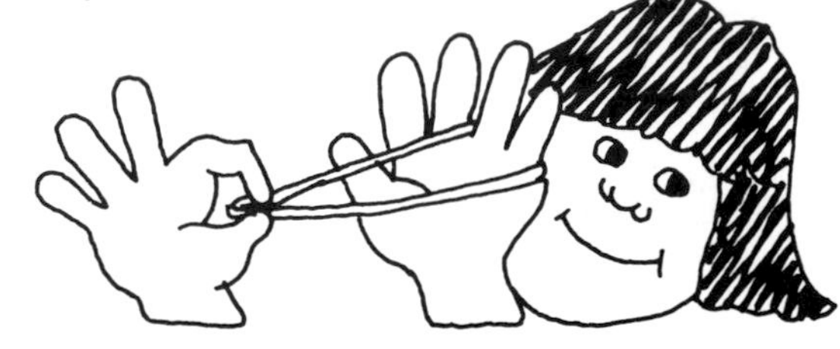

Then turn your hand back palm down, BUT as you do it, make a loose fist and stick your other 2 fingers under the band like this. This is the part that needs practice.

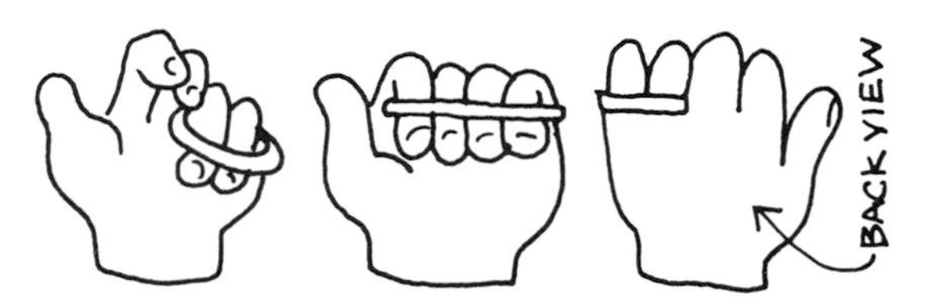

When you straighten out your fingers, the rubber band will leap to your other 2 fingers!

When you do this trick, you are demonstrating a topological principal involving insides and outsides. (Remember topology?) Watch the rubber band closely as you do the trick.

THE GREAT LOOP AND JACKET TRICK

Save this trick for the last. It is almost pure topology and very little magic. But it will confound your audience and secure your place among the all-time magic greats in their minds.

Have your assistant face the audience. She should have on a jacket, with plenty of room in it, and a 2 metre long piece of thick yarn tied into a loop over one arm, as shown. That hand should be in her pocket.

Without permitting your assistant to remove her hand from her pocket, you will now remove the string loop from her arm without untying it. Tell your audience that.

"Impossible," they will say. You may get sneers or sniggers. Let them carry on while you do this:

The SHRINKING 10p coin

First, trace around a 5p coin on a piece of paper about this size. Cut out the circle you traced.

Then say to your audience:

"Which of you can push a 10p through this hole without tearing the paper?"

Unless 1 of them has already seen this trick, or is another mathematician in disguise, they won't be able to do it.
But you will.

Smile at them comfortingly and fold the paper in half, like this.

Place the 10p coin in the fold so it's sticking through a little, like this.

Hold the corners of the paper and raise them a little, like this.

The hole will open up and the coin will fall through!

And there you have it, ladies and gentlemen, the 10p that shrinks to the size of a 5p!

(Diameters aren't always what you think they are.)

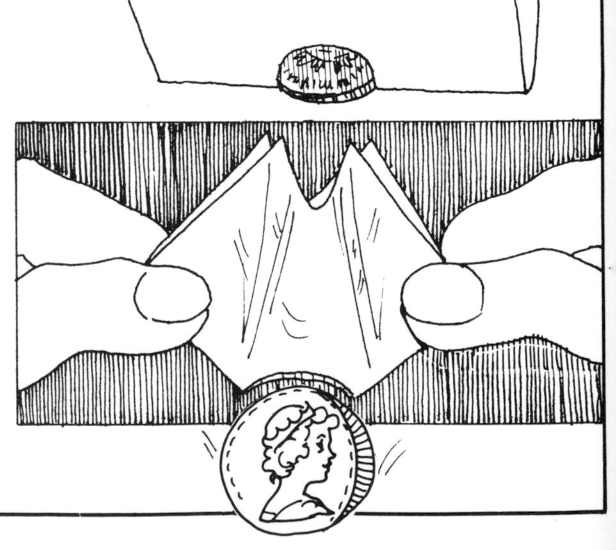

How to Always Be a Winner

It's not whether you win or lose that's important.
It's how you play the game.

You've heard *that* one before.
Probably someone who always wins made it up.

Mathematical games are different from most.
It is usually possible to figure out *how* to win them *every time.*
Then you can decide for yourself
whether what's important about the game is to win.

Here are some strategy games that can all be figured out.
Play with a friend.
Then it's easier to figure out how to win.

Another good thing about mathematical games.
If you get tired of the rules, you can change them.

From now on, if you aren't a winner,
there is no one to blame but yourself.

POISON – A FRIENDLY GAME

You need:

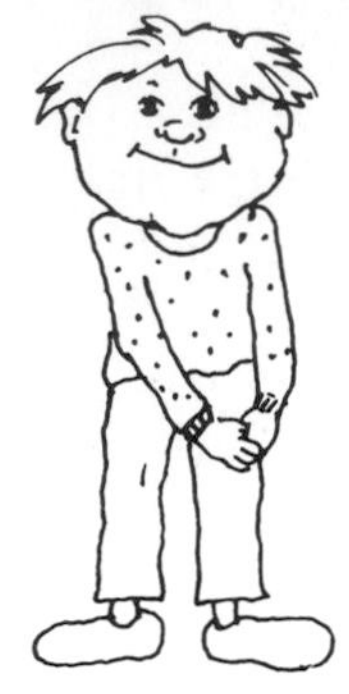

A friend,

12 things that are the same — like beans, or nails, or bottlecaps and

one more thing that is different — the *poison*.

Say to your friend:

"How about a friendly game of *poison?*"

Take turns.

When your turn comes you must take away 1 thing, or 2 things, until only the poison is left.

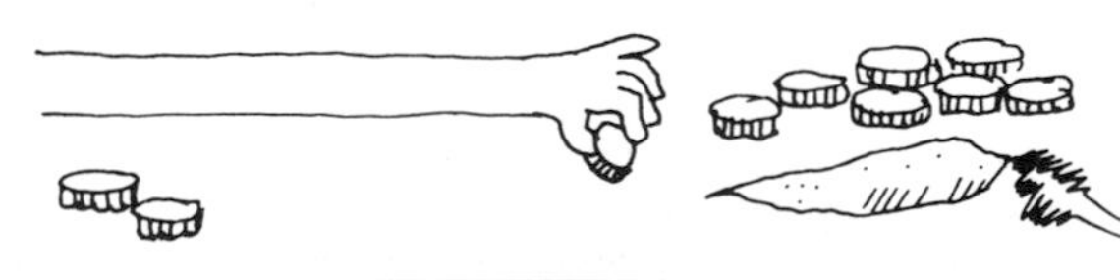

Whoever takes away the poison, *dies*.

How can you always avoid the poison?

You'll have to figure that out. (We can't tell you *everything!* But it's possible.)

Some hints. (Well, questions, really.)

Is it better to go 1st or 2nd?

What would happen if there were a different number of things?

How would it be if you could take away 1 or 2 or 3 things?

If you play enough, you'll figure it out.

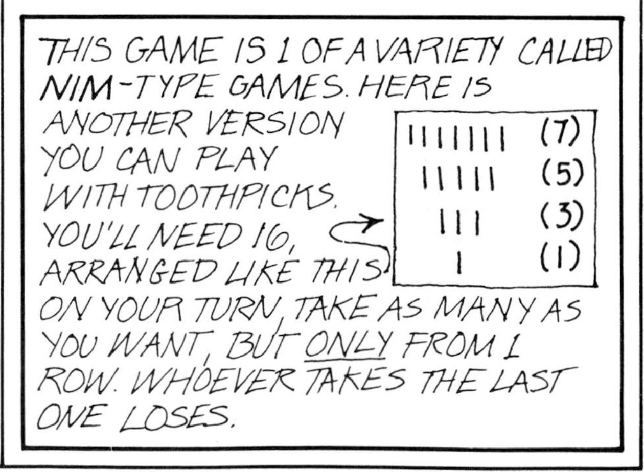

RACE FOR 20

Do you know how it feels when you're squashed in the back seat of the car with your brother and sister and the 3 of you have been real noisy and you're about to get in trouble? And you're not even half-way to where you're going?

Try this game. Any number can play, but it's best for 2 people. Because then you can figure out how to always be a winner.

It goes like this:

It's a counting game.

Whoever gets 20 wins.

You take turns.

When it's your turn, you may count 1 or 2 numbers.

So the first person says, "1" or "1, 2." And the second continues with 1 or 2 more numbers.

Try it. If there are more than 2 of you, take turns and play the winners. Keep track of how many games each wins.

peculiar is as peculiar does
HI!
I'VE ALWAYS FELT A LITTLE PECULIAR. I APPEAR AT THE STRANGEST TIMES AND NO ONE KNOWS WHY.
6174
I'M THE ONLY NUMBER THAT SHOWS UP LIKE THIS.
HERE'S HOW YOU CAN MAKE ME HAPPEN
PICK 4 DIFFERENT NUMBERS FROM 0 TO 9 .... 7 8 2 3
• ARRANGE THEM TO MAKE THE LARGEST NUMBER POSSIBLE. 8732
• NOW ARRANGE THEM TO MAKE THE SMALLEST NUMBER POSSIBLE 2378
• SUBTRACT THE SMALL NUMBER FROM THE LARGE ONE. .... 8732 −2378 6354
• GOOD!
ALREADY I THINK SOMETHING'S PECULIAR.
• NOW, TAKE THE ANSWER AND ARRANGE THOSE NUMBERS TO MAKE THE LARGEST NUMBER POSSIBLE. 6543
• AND THE SMALLEST .... −3456
• SUBTRACT 3087
8730 −0378 8352
8532 −2358 6174
AND THERE I AM!
TRY IT. I'LL ALWAYS TURN UP, EVENTUALLY. I MAY BE PECULIAR, BUT I'M DEPENDABLE.

Here is the playing field. Start with 4 dots in each direction. (Later you can add more.)

Draw it on any piece of paper.

You'll also need a friend.

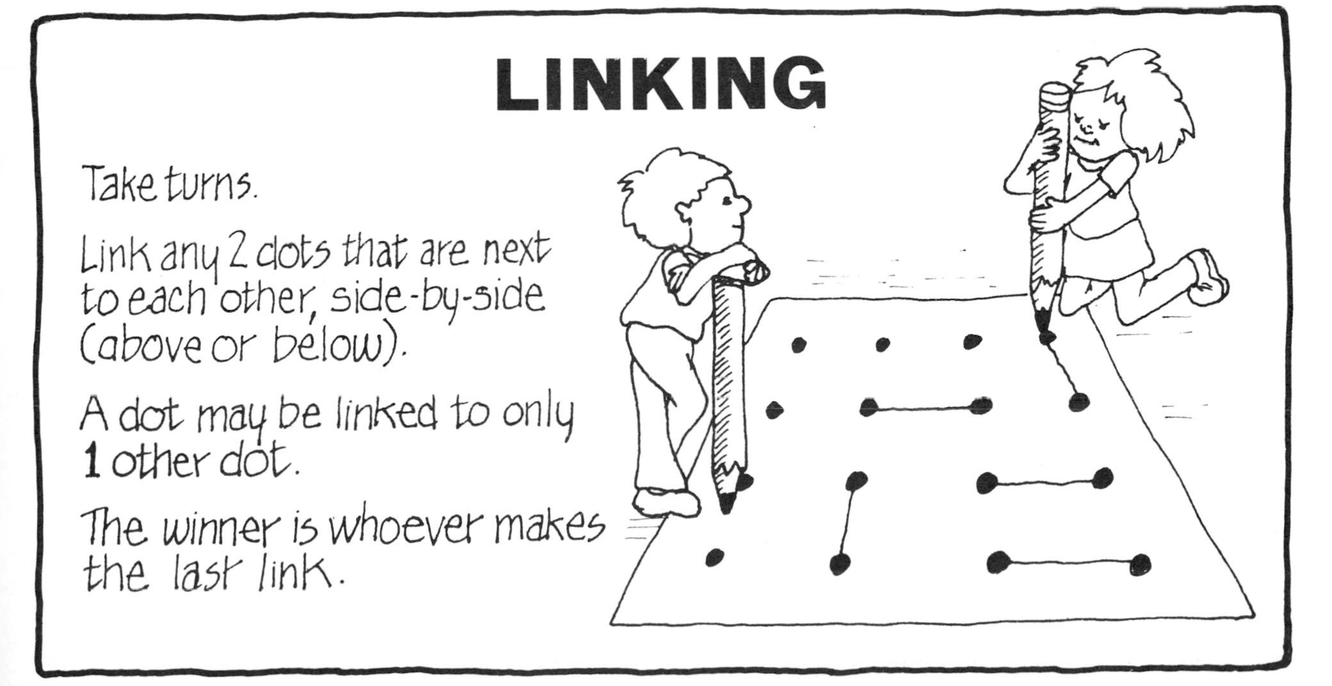

LINKING

Take turns.

Link any 2 dots that are next to each other, side-by-side (above or below).

A dot may be linked to only **1** other dot.

The winner is whoever makes the last link.

UP RIGHT

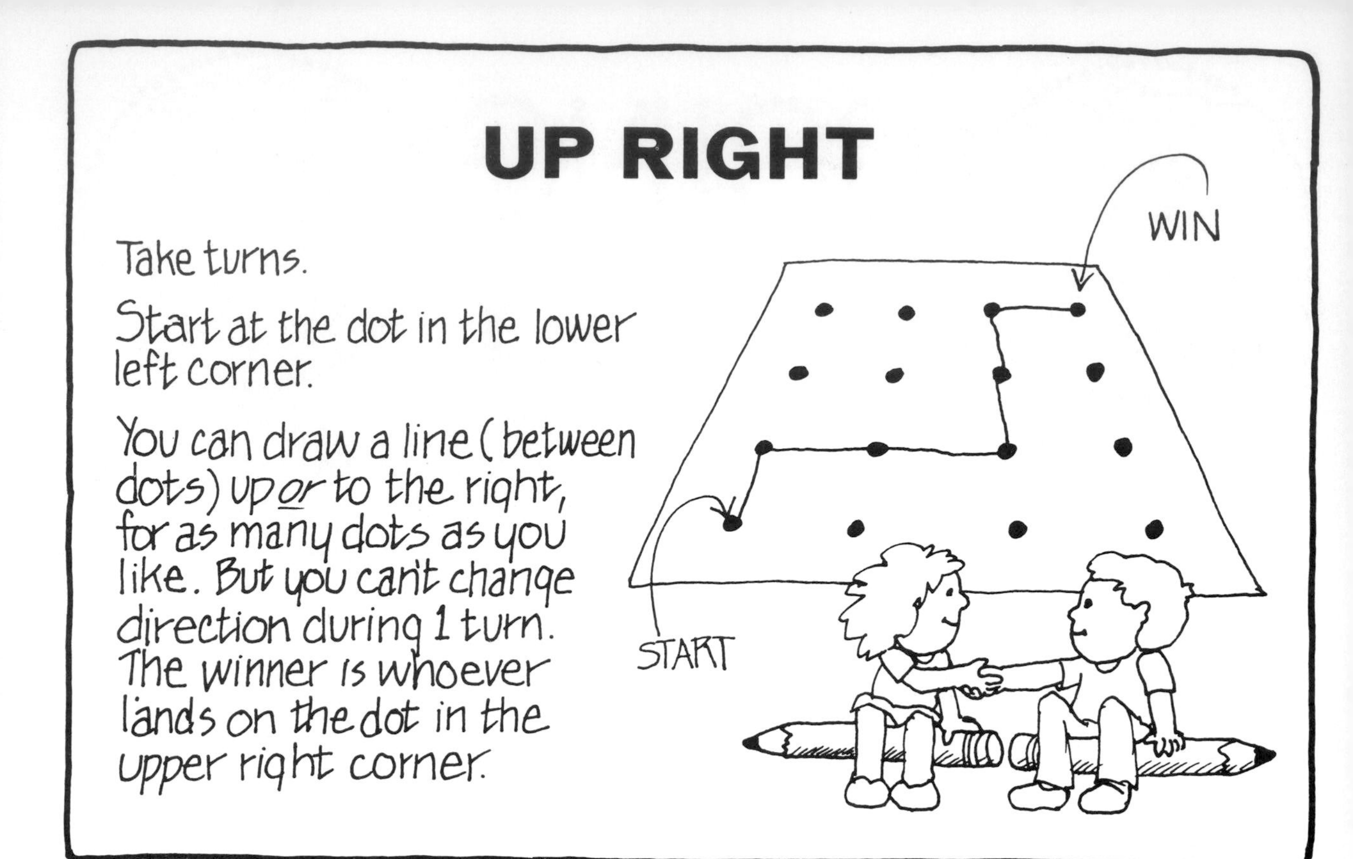

Take turns.

Start at the dot in the lower left corner.

You can draw a line (between dots) up *or* to the right, for as many dots as you like. But you can't change direction during 1 turn. The winner is whoever lands on the dot in the upper right corner.

CREEP

Take turns.

You may draw a line any length across, up, down, or diagonally.

You may not cross another line or close the shape or turn a corner on 1 turn.

You have to draw your line from either end of what is already there. (Straight lines only.)

Winner is whoever draws the last possible line.

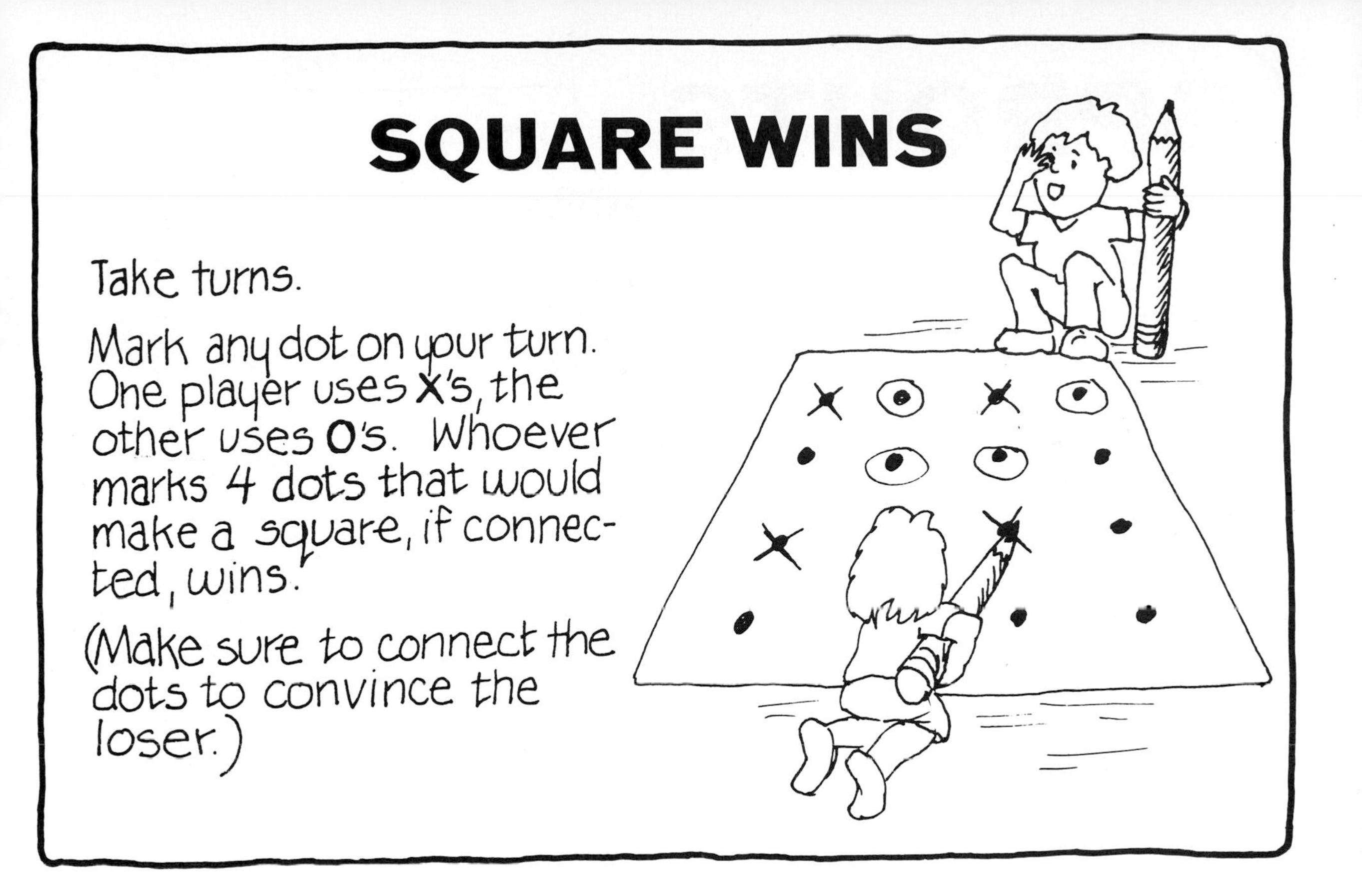

SQUARE WINS

Take turns.

Mark any dot on your turn. One player uses X's, the other uses O's. Whoever marks 4 dots that would make a square, if connected, wins.

(Make sure to connect the dots to convince the loser.)

THINK SMALL

All of these games involve strategy. If you know the strategy you can *always* win. One way to get a good look at the strategy is to see what happens when there are fewer dots.

Like in the game "Linking," if there were 4 dots instead of 16 it would be a sure win if you went second.

What if there were 6 dots?
Then you'd win only if you went first.

What about 8 dots?
See that pattern?

Work your way up to 16.

SPROUTS

A topological network game. Or, in plain English, a game drawing points and lines.

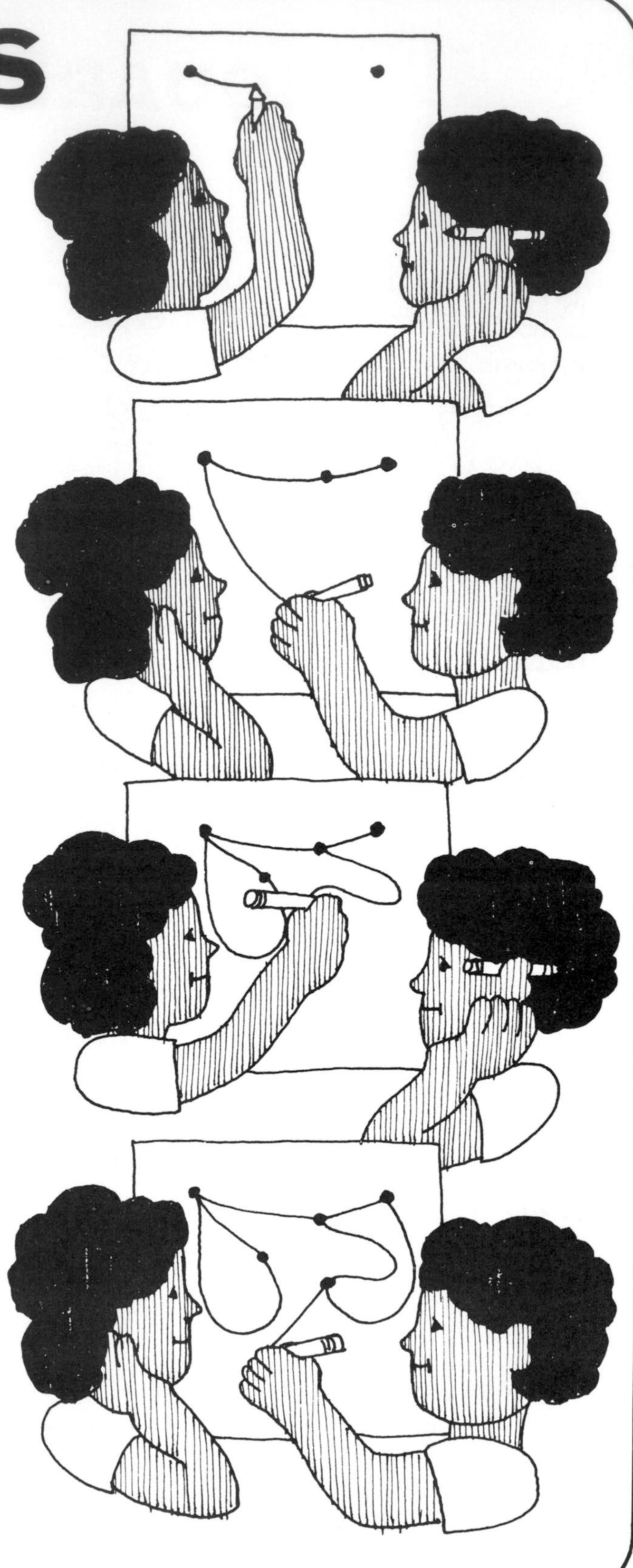

Start with 2 points, and take turns drawing lines by these rules:

A line must start and end at a point. (Curved lines are okay, and you can draw a loop and end at the same point you started at.)

After you draw a line, you must mark a new point somewhere on it.

No line can cross itself or another line, or pass through any point.

No point can have more than 3 lines ending there.

The winner is the last person able to play.

This game was invented by 2 British mathematicians. You might have known, huh?

How long could a game continue?

What would happen if you started with 3 or 4 points?

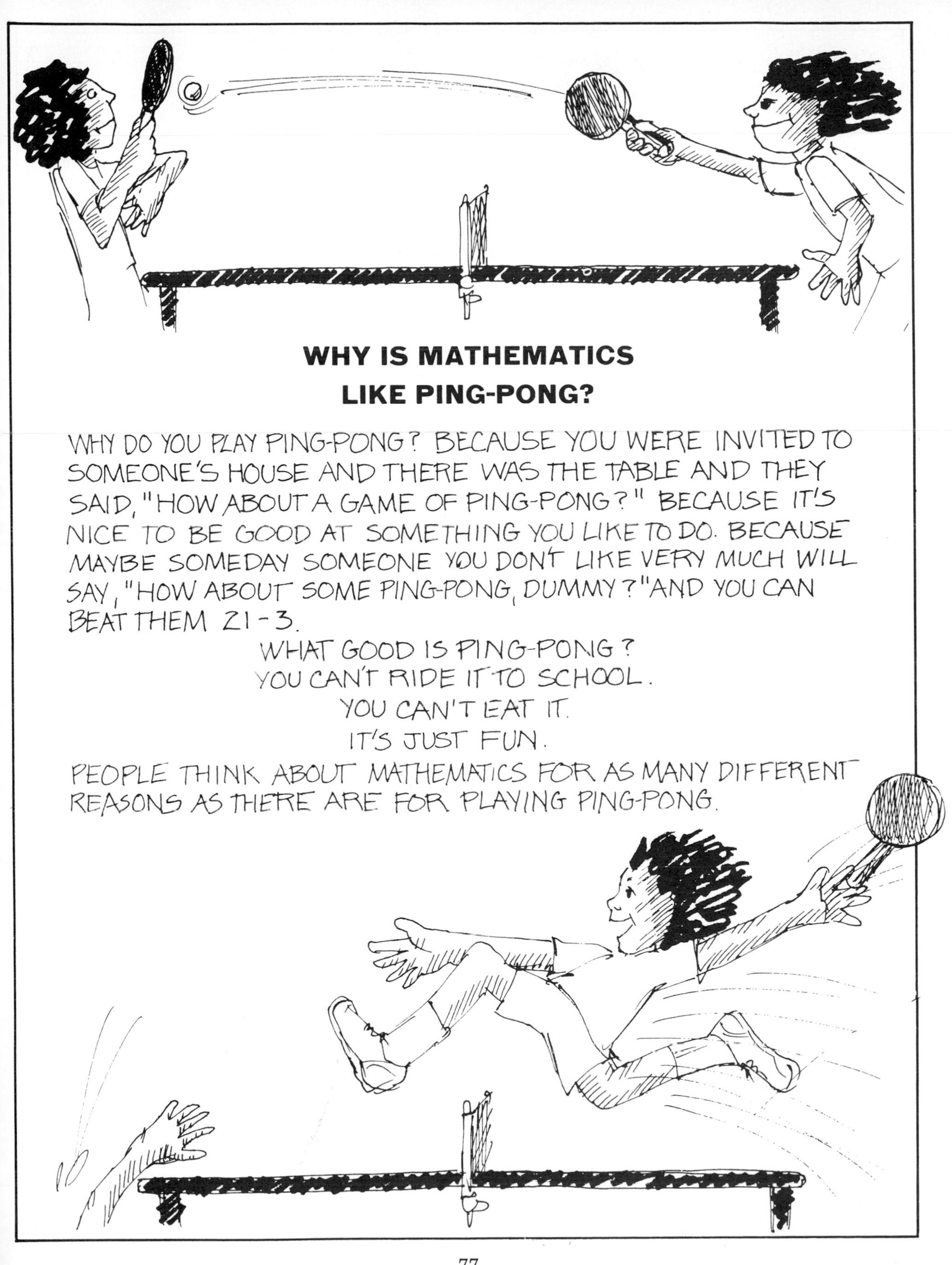
WHY IS MATHEMATICS
LIKE PING-PONG?
WHY DO YOU PLAY PING-PONG? BECAUSE YOU WERE INVITED TO SOMEONE'S HOUSE AND THERE WAS THE TABLE AND THEY SAID, "HOW ABOUT A GAME OF PING-PONG?" BECAUSE IT'S NICE TO BE GOOD AT SOMETHING YOU LIKE TO DO. BECAUSE MAYBE SOMEDAY SOMEONE YOU DON'T LIKE VERY MUCH WILL SAY, "HOW ABOUT SOME PING-PONG, DUMMY?" AND YOU CAN BEAT THEM 21-3.
WHAT GOOD IS PING-PONG?
YOU CAN'T RIDE IT TO SCHOOL.
YOU CAN'T EAT IT.
IT'S JUST FUN.
PEOPLE THINK ABOUT MATHEMATICS FOR AS MANY DIFFERENT REASONS AS THERE ARE FOR PLAYING PING-PONG.

How Many Sides Does a Banana Have?

Bananas in a mathematics book?
Why not?
Mathematics lurks everywhere.
Even in bananas.

Also in apples, cabbages, onions,
tin cans, jars, glasses.
All over the place.

It's enough to make you sick.

HOW MANY SIDES DOES A BANANA HAVE?

Before you go rummaging around in the kitchen, think about that question. Can you picture how many sides a banana has? If the shops are closed and there isn't a banana in the kitchen, you'll have to use your memory anyway.

You could call your best friend and see if there is a banana at their house.

Do all bananas have the same number of sides? Do bananas even *have* sides? Is there a constant banana pattern?

But don't stop at the banana. You're just getting started. There are patterns in lots of foods. Don't ignore them. There are amazing examples of *symmetry* in the kitchen. Enough to boggle the mind.

Take an apple. You know what it looks like if you cut it like this.

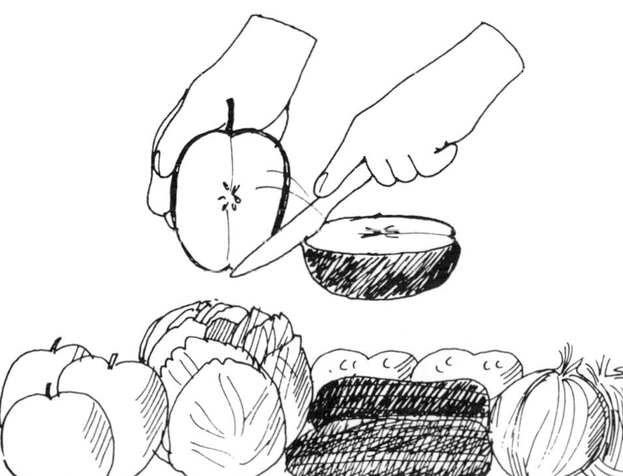

But what if you cut it like this? Can you predict what it will look like inside? What other foods make patterns like the apple?

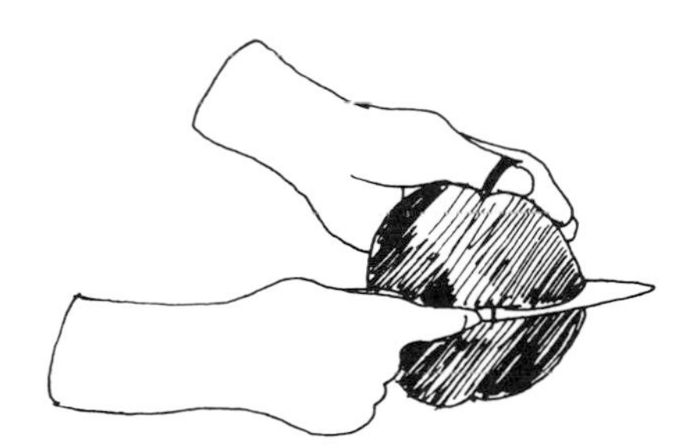

Start hanging around the kitchen. When someone is preparing dinner, ask to cut the vegetables. Try cutting onions both ways. Or cabbages, cucumbers or tomatoes. Try fruit. You won't believe the symmetry.

MORE THAN ONE WAY
(to slice a banana)

You thought we were through with bananas, didn't you? Here's another banana experiment for you to try the next time you are asked to help make the fruit salad.

Look at the drawing. You can slice a banana with its skin on —

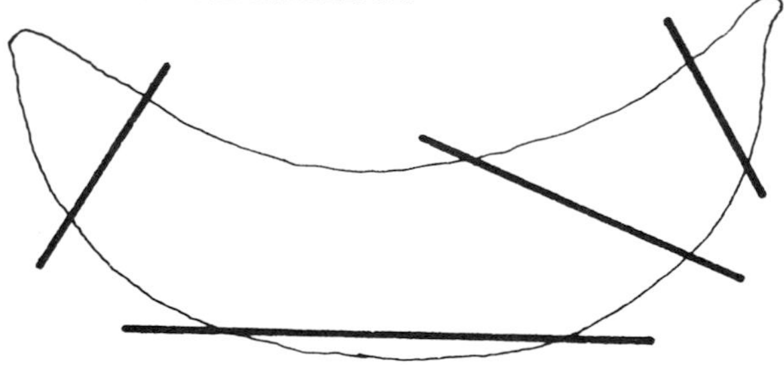

and make all these slice shapes.

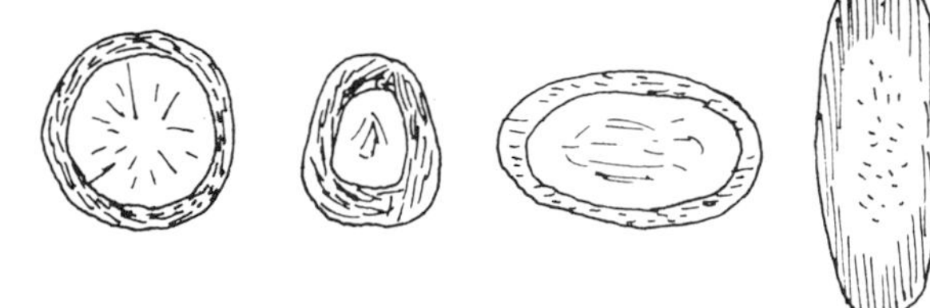

Which shapes go with which slices?

In the event someone comes along and demands to know why you are cutting up a perfectly good banana in such a crazy way, you can tell them about your investigation.

You can also remark casually that this experiment was first conducted by a Greek mathematician of the third century B.C., named Apollonius, who wrote a book called *The Conics*, which was all about slicing cones. (Apollonius might have used bananas, but . . .)

Apollonius found that if you slice a cone like this, the shape you get is a circle.

But if you slice it like this, the shape you get is an *ellipse*.

He sliced cones in other ways too. He got other curves called *hyperbolas* and *parabolas*.

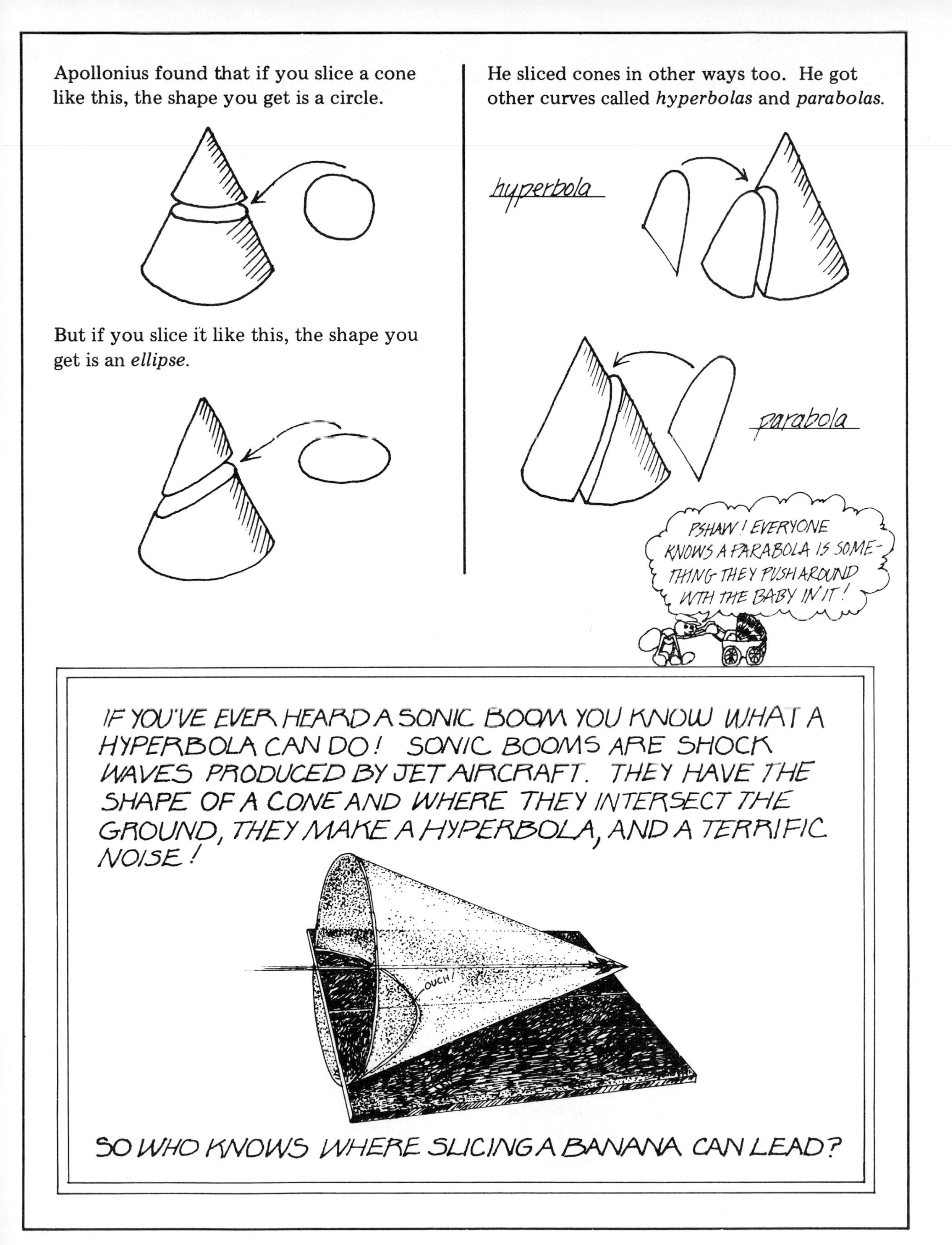

More Than You Probably Want To Know About Symmetry

Mathematicians invented lots of stuff to fool around with. But they didn't invent symmetry. It's all over the place. They just stumbled on it. Chances are, if the mathematicians hadn't noticed all the symmetry around, someone else would have. Maybe dentists. Symmetry is pretty hard *not* to notice. You might try *not* noticing symmetry for a while. Don't look at aeroplanes. Don't look at motorcars. Try not to notice any dogs or cats. In fact, you could *not* look at just about anything and probably miss a lot of symmetry.

The mathematicians didn't invent symmetry. But it was just like them to give a fancy name to something that was there from the beginning.

Some shapes have *mirror symmetry*, they say. Such shapes have at least 1 *line of symmetry*, like the butterfly . . .

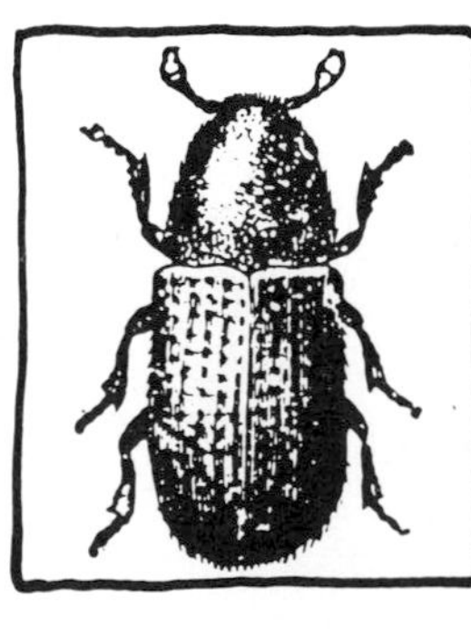

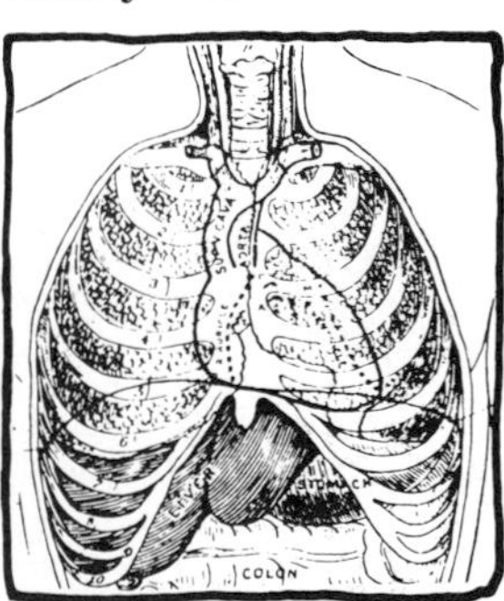

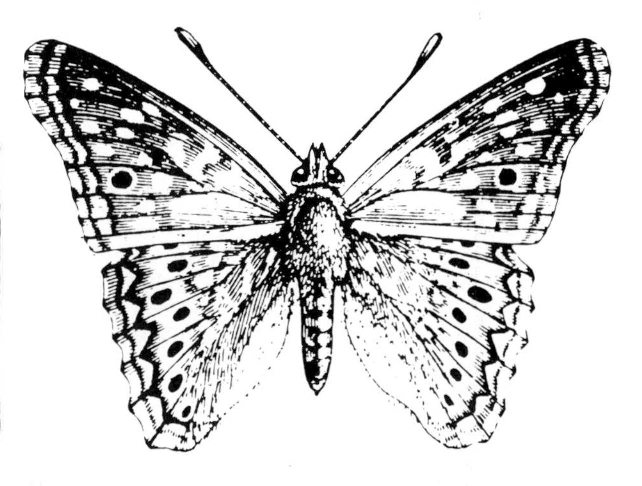

Or 2 lines of symmetry, like the letter H.

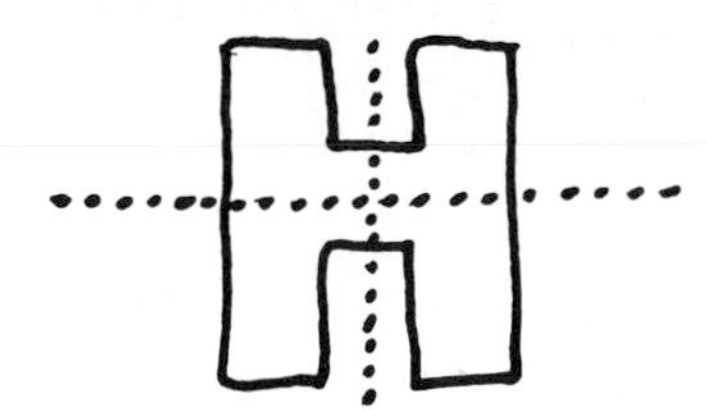

Some shapes have *rotational symmetry* and have a *point of symmetry*, which means you can turn the shape less than 1 full turn and it will look the same as when it was right side up.

Some shapes have *both* kinds of symmetry.

QUESTION: WHERE DOES 10 PLUS 3 EQUAL 1?
IS THERE A CLOCK IN YOUR KITCHEN? IF YOU ADD 3 HOURS ON TO 10 O'CLOCK, WHERE DO YOU LAND?
IF I ADD 3 HOURSH ON TO 10 O'CLOCK, I LAND IN LOTSH OF TROUBLE WHEN I GET HOME! (BURP!)
SO 10+3=1 IN THE KITCHEN. SO DOES 11+2 AND 9+4.
This clock arithmetic is not just silly stuff. Some mathematicians like it a lot. They call it **modulo arithmetic** and 1 advantage is that you don't have to count higher than 12! (One disadvantage is that you get the wrong answer if you do your regular arithmetic this way.)
SUPPOSE THE CLOCK LOOKED LIKE THIS. (THIS CLOCK HAS 6 NUMBERS ON IT. IT'S A MODULAR 6 SYSTEM.) THEN 4+2=0 AND 3+5=2. JUST COUNT AROUND THE CLOCK TO GET THE ANSWERS.
LOOKING AT THESE SYSTEMS INTERESTS SOME MATHEMATICIANS. IT'S JUST A DIFFERENT WAY TO APPROACH MATHS — WITH A DIFFERENT SET OF RULES.

QUESTION: WHEN DOES 3 PLUS 1 NOT EQUAL 4?
In the kitchen again.
HUH?
SALT
Three tablespoons of water plus 1 tablespoon of salt do not equal 4 tablespoons of salt water.
SALT
THE POPCORN KID ASKS: HOW MANY PIECES OF POPCORN WOULD FILL THE REFRIG-ERATOR?

If you have tried the "Great Dishes Scheme" on page 35 and it didn't work, but you're still doing those dishes, here is a mathematical escape that will probably work at least once. (You may not get away with it more times than that, so use it when you really need it.)

DRYING DISHES

Take a look at the glasses. If you have read the first part of this book, you already know something about those glasses besides that they need a lot of wiping. Answer this question:

Which measures more, the height of the glass, or around the top?

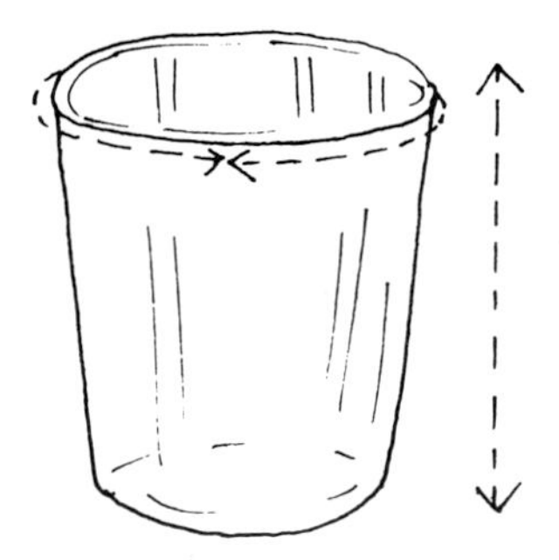

If you're not sure, use the tea towel to measure it. Try different glasses. You probably won't find any that are taller than they are around. You also won't find very many people who can tell that just by looking. Get the idea?

Now line up 4 glasses. Then choose your victim. Ask them to choose which one they think is taller than it is around. Bet them your turn at drying they can't find one.

Then hand over the towel.

INFINITY IS NOT A PLACE

Infinity is not a town. Or any other place. Here is another thing infinity isn't. It isn't the biggest number ever, or the biggest anything else. In fact, infinity isn't any *thing* at all — it's an idea. Something that is infinite goes on forever. It has no edges, and no stopping place.

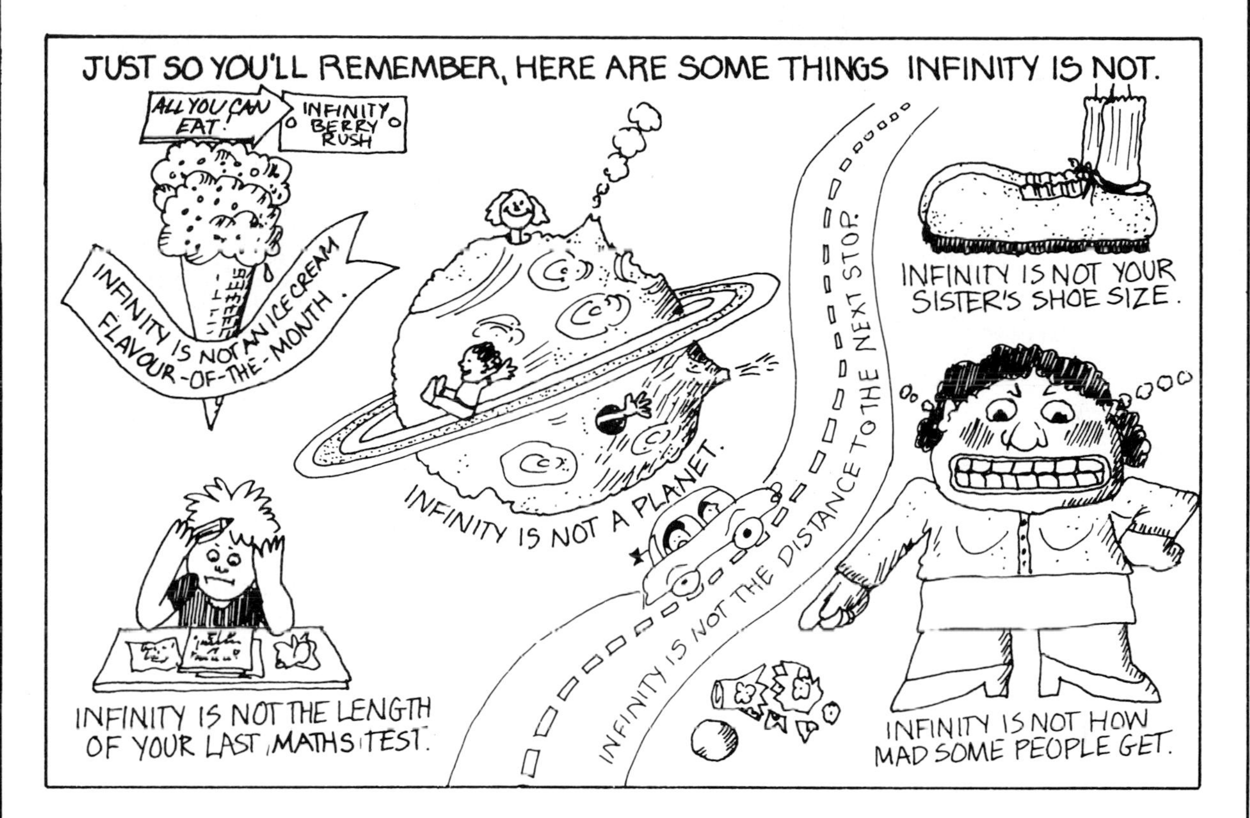

Here is something infinity is: infinity is probably the hardest idea in this book. That's because you can't see it or feel it or draw a picture of it. And it isn't like anything else.

It does have a symbol, which looks like this:

And maybe if you let the idea roll around in your head for a while, and every once in a while give it a turn or 2, you'll begin to get a *sense* of what infinity is.

And then you can be pretty proud of yourself. Because the best mathematician in the world can't do any better than that.

PI
Hi, I'm pi!
I'm a fast-talking, quick-stepping number found everywhere there is anything round....
But you can never find all of me. I said I was quick-stepping, didn't I? You can get close. You can even find me in a drum.
Measure around the edge and then across the top. Divide the two numbers and don't ever stop.
I hate long division.
It will take a while. Mathematicians call this figuring finding pi (the ratio of the circumference and diameter of any circle). They write me like this: π

I'm a little bit larger than 3.
But smaller than 4.
Most people call me **3.14**, which is a decimal number....
.....But actually I go on and on and I never end — and I never repeat. I am also infinite.
Here's just a part of me :
3.1415926535897932384626433832
79502884197169399375105820974
9445923078164062862089986280
348253421170679..etc. etc. etc......
Decimal numbers which go forever and never repeat are called **irrational** numbers.

The Art of Probably

By now you should be getting a few mathematical muscles.
Here is where you can put them to use.

Do you think there is a chance
that there will be an earthquake in 1 minute?
If the answer is *yes*,
then you've got no business sitting around looking at this book.
If the answer is *no*,
then you've got your own theory of chance.

What's that?
It's the thing that keeps you from taking a raincoat
on a sunny day.
It keeps you from worrying that your mum
has joined a rock group and has gone off on a world tour
instead of getting supper.
You use it all the time in ways you don't even think about.

Mathematicians have their own ideas
about what might or might not happen.
They call them *mathematical theories of probability*.

But, you can just call it the art of making good guesses.

GUESSING RIGHT

(Or the 3p of probability)

Toss a penny. The mathematical theory of probability for tossing pennies says that the chance of getting heads is 50-50, or 1 in 2, or ½. You already knew that, huh?

But a penny doesn't *always* come up heads exactly ½ the time you toss it. And that fact is what makes games of chance fun to play and some people into gamblers. (If it did come up heads exactly ½ the time, you wouldn't be interested in tossing it in the first place.)

Try this. Toss a penny and a 2p. What is the chance you will toss 2 heads? Here are the possibilities:

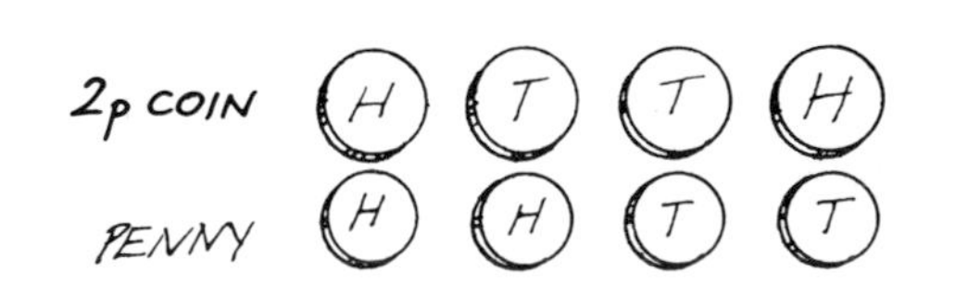

There are 4 ways for the coins to turn up. And 2 heads comes up in only 1 of those 4 ways. The mathematical theory of probability for tossing pennies and 2p coins says that if both coins are tossed, the chance that heads will come up on both is 1 out of 4, or ¼.

Keep track of your tosses on a chart like this. How close to the theory do your tosses come?

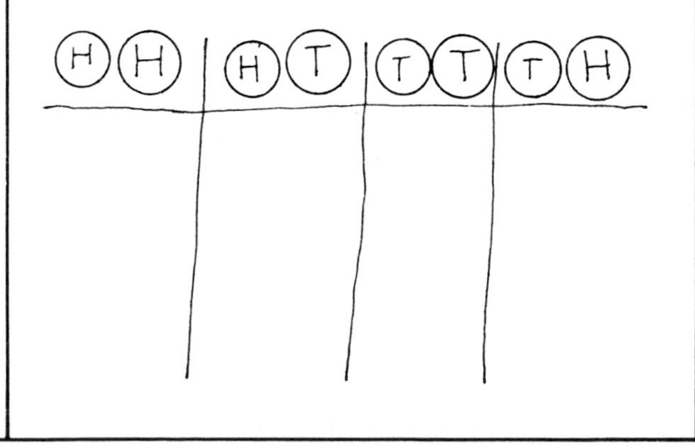

WHAT'S THE CHANCE

of being invited to 2 Birthday Parties in 1 Day?

Not bad, if you know at least 30 people who have birthday parties every year. Like your class at school. In any group of 30 people, there is a better than 2 to 1 chance that 2 people will have the same birthday.

Mathematicians who study probability theory (and like birthday parties) have proven this to be true.

Try it yourself. Take a poll. Ask people when their birthdays are and stop when you find 2 with the same one. Sometimes it happens right away.

Sometimes it takes a long time.

But if you take the poll *enough times*, the average number of people you have to ask will get very close to 30. If you get sick of asking people when their birthdays are before you get an average of 30, you'll just have to take our word for it.

Are there more birthdays in some months than others? Are the chances that 2 people will have the same birthday better in June than in December?

THE BIRTHDAY INSURANCE COMPANY

How would you like to start an insurance business?

Suppose you sold insurance to people who wanted to insure that it wouldn't rain on their birthdays.

And if it did they'd collect £5.

Most adults have 1 form of insurance or another. Car insurance. House insurance. Health insurance. Life insurance.

Insurance companies rely on probability theory to decide how much to charge. They use lots and lots of statistics.

What you need to know to insure un-rainy birthdays is:

How many days does it rain in a year? When are those days likely to be?

Maybe people with birthdays in February would pay more than those with birthdays in June?

Check an almanac for weather information.

How much would you charge?

How many people would you need to buy the insurance so you wouldn't lose money?

IS THIS BUSINESS POSSIBLE?

Here is a good game. It depends on knowing a little something about probability as well as not being too much of a pig.

You need 2 dice, a friend, and a paper and pencil (unless you are terrific at adding numbers in your head).

You roll the dice and add up what they say. The idea is to get to 100. You don't have to take turns. You keep rolling as long as you want. BUT:

If a 1 comes up on 1 of the dice, you lose your count for that turn.

If a 1 comes up on both dice, your total goes back to 0. (Even if you were at 98!) And anytime you throw a 1, you lose your turn.

It helps a lot to know how to add. But it helps even more if you can predict how often 1's will come up. What is the probability of throwing one 1? What is the probability of throwing snake eyes (two 1's)?

What is a lucky streak? Do you know one when you have it?

ALPHABETICAL PROBABILITY

There is even an alphabetical theory of probability. Want to know what it says? That's good, because here it comes:

The letter of the alphabet that occurs most often in written English is the letter E. T, A, O, and N are the next most frequent. Letters that are used the least are Q, Z, K, X, and J.

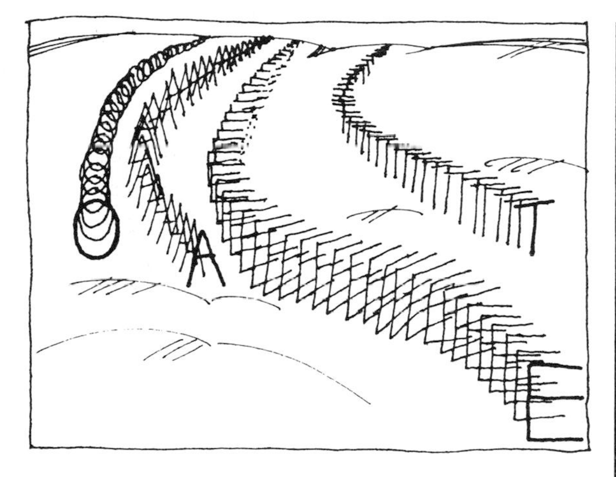

Try it out for yourself. Make up a chart which has a column for each letter. Then pick a page in this book and tally each time a letter appears.

When you find out how often each letter occurs, you are making a *frequency distribution.* Mathematicians have used frequency distributions to help crack codes. You can do the same thing with cryptograms. They're a kind of puzzle in which each letter stands for another letter (a stands for b, b stands for c, and so forth). It's like a code.

Ask a friend to write you a message using a cryptogram. Then see if you can figure out the code by using your frequency distribution.

THIS IS ODD. DO YOU KNOW WHY? TRY AND THINK OF WHAT IT IS. GOOD LUCK!

WHAT'S ODD ABOUT THE WORDS IN THIS BOX?

The sentence at the bottom of this page
is true.

WHEN IS AN ANSWER NO FUN AT ALL?

Look at it this way. Once you've got the answer to a mathematical problem, you don't have the problem anymore. If you're trying to get through 100 problems in your maths book, that might sound just fine.

But to a mathematician, it's a little like taking the last good suck on a straw full of chocolate milkshake. (The one just before it starts making that gurgling sound.) It's too bad there isn't any more.

Which is very close to where you are in this book. Almost finished.

Do you feel a *little less* like a mathematical weakling? If you're sorry it's almost over, then you are certainly no mathematical weakling and you should cheer up. The world is full of mathematical problems and puzzles to solve, remember?

The sentence at the top of this page
is false.